KINNAIRD HEAD LIGHTHOUSE

AN ILLUSTRATED HISTORY

Michael A. W. Strachan

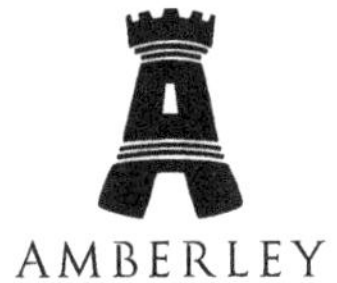

AMBERLEY

Acknowledgements

First and foremost, the author wishes to thank Lynda McGuigan, Manager of the Museum of Scottish Lighthouses, for granting permission to use many important images from the Museum's Recognised Collection of National Significance in the production of this book. Were it not for that, or indeed her decision to reinstate me to the Lighthouse Museum at Kinnaird Head, this book would not have been written.

Special thanks to The Hon. Mrs Katharine Nicolson DL for kindly allowing me to visit her home to view and reproduce paintings of her ancestors. The author also wishes to thank Alison Metcalfe at the National Library of Scotland for advice offered on collections prior to my visit, and also to Fiona Holmes at the Northern Lighthouse Board for facilitating answers to my many questions on the modern service.

The author is particularly grateful to those who shared their memories of the service for the purpose of this book, including: Margaret Stewart; Sidney Scott; Brian and Janet Petrie; Duncan McIntosh; Gordon Stewart; John Boath and the Shanks family. The author wishes to thank all those who have given permission to use their images in this book, who have been credited throughout – particularly Ian Cowe, whose stunning image of Kinnaird Head graces the front cover of this title.

Final thanks to Lynne Strachan and Kevin Watt for proofreading the text for this book.

Written for all my friends and colleagues at the Museum of Scottish Lighthouses 2012–14, 2015–19. And also for my friends at the Counters who kept me going in exile, 2014–15!

First published 2019

Amberley Publishing
The Hill, Stroud
Gloucestershire, GL5 4EP

www.amberleybooks.com

British Library Cataloguing in Publication Data.
A catalogue record for this book is available from the British Library.

ISBN 978 1 4456 8251 8 (print)
ISBN 978 1 4456 8252 5 (ebook)

Typesetting by Aura Technology and Software Services, India.
Printed in Great Britain.

Contents

Introduction

On the extreme north-east point of the Scottish mainland lies the promontory of Kinnaird Head, which has been noted through history as a natural marker for seafarers as well as a position of strength on the land. Its name, taken from the Gaelic 'An Ceann Àrd', literally means 'High Headland' – a dominant feature on the land first recorded in about AD 150 by the Greco-Roman mathematician and geographer Ptolemy as 'Taizalum Promontoriam'. It is clear, therefore, that Kinnaird Head has always been an important marker for mariners navigating that treacherous part of the rocky coast.

Many centuries later it was the wealth from the seas that brought Kinnaird Head to greater prominence when Sir Alexander Fraser, 8th Laird of Philorth, chose the imposing headland to build his new castle in 1570. It was built there to be seen as the centre-point and power base of his ambitious plan to establish his new town of Fraserburgh and oversee the investments and improvements in the port he hoped would make his fortune. When that ambition failed (along with Scotland's forgotten university) the castle should have failed with it to become just another pile of picturesque ruins on Scotland's coast. Kinnaird Head, though, as this book will show, has always been the exception to the rule. It is a site which has constantly adapted and, against all odds, still stands today.

The castle, then very close to ruin, was redeveloped and reinvented in 1787 when it underwent its first major transition to become the Northern Lighthouse Board's first light. This was an identity change that again made the castle the heart of the town serving, as it did, the local fishermen and mariners, many of whom had lost fathers and brothers in the pursuit of their livelihoods. Although the old tower was a castle for 217 years and only a lighthouse for 204, this book will predominantly focus on that fascinating lighthouse history. The story of Kinnaird Head is the story of the NLB. This is not purely because of its status as the first, but because it was visited by every member of the Stevenson dynasty over their 150-year service and has seen every change and benefit of their collective technical and engineering genius. While much time will be spent covering the Stevensons' periodic punctuations in Kinnaird Head's timeline, the book will also highlight the age of the lightkeeper during their 204 years unbroken vigil at the station. The book will follow them from James Park switching on the light in 1787, to Jim Oliver switching it off for the last time in 1991.

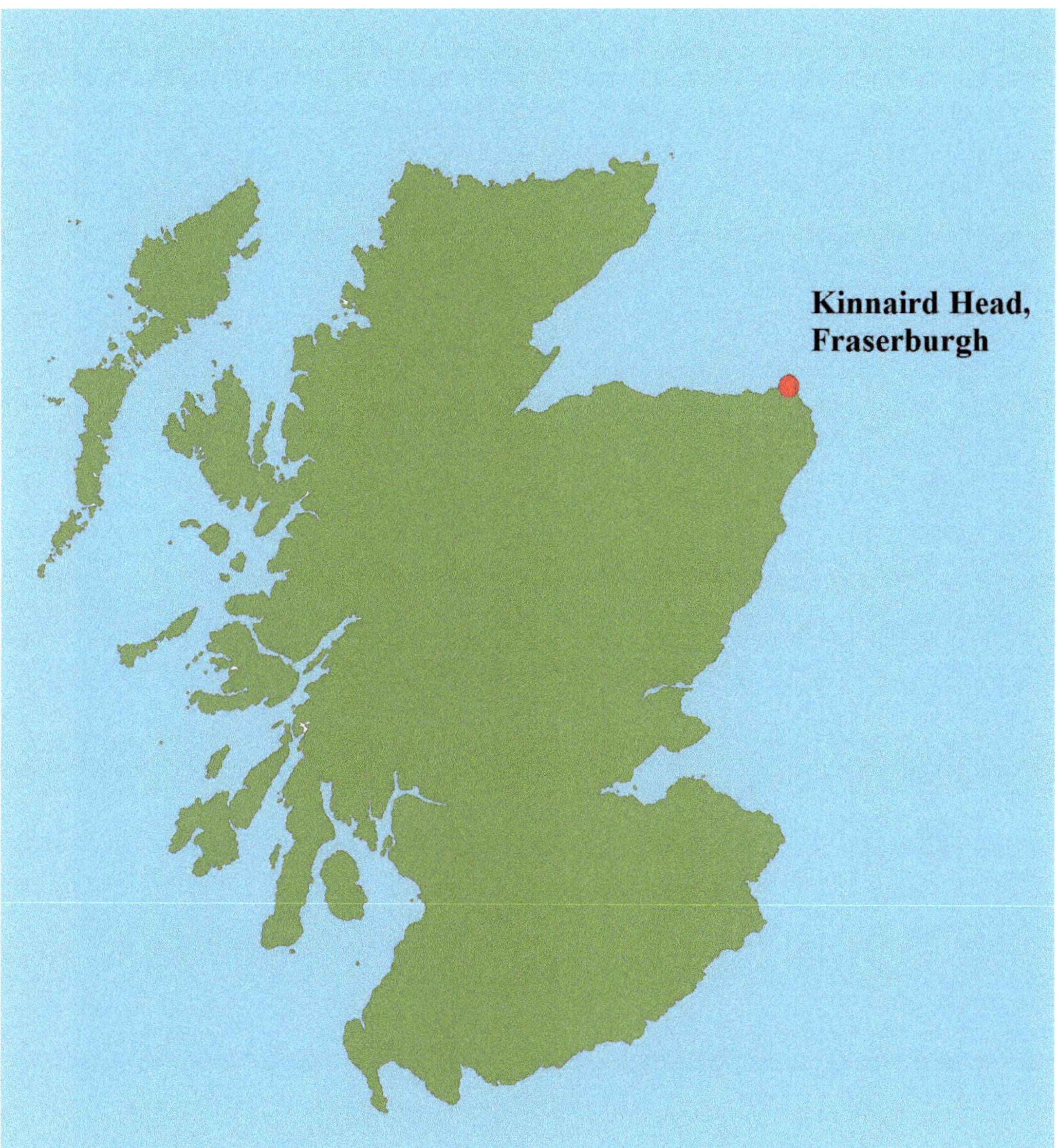

Kinnaird Head, Fraserburgh, is located on the north-eastern coast of Scotland.

The book will then conclude in the present day, exploring how Kinnaird Head once again became the exception to the rule with its transformation into a museum. While all other lighthouses went through automation – or worse still decommissioning – the old tower at Kinnaird escaped that painful process by being purposely preserved as a manned lighthouse to become part of the Museum of Scottish Lighthouses.

In this new capacity, the lighthouse has maintained its significance and strategic importance to the town as it faced new economic challenges with the decline of the

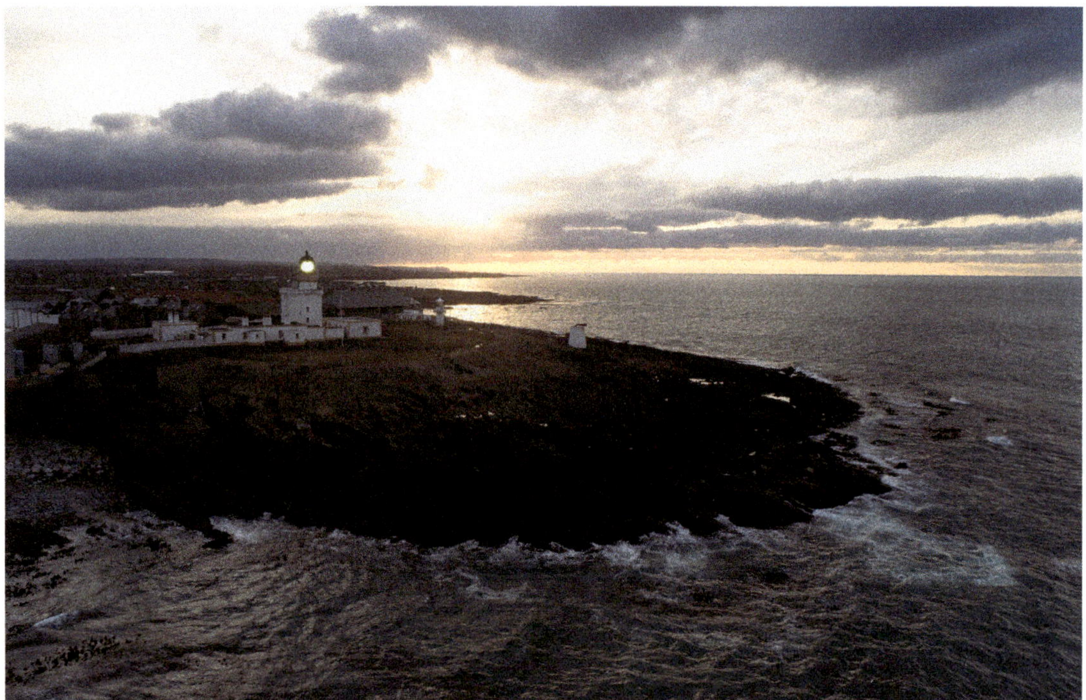

The promontory of Kinnaird Head provided an imposing headland which was a recognisable feature on the coast long before the lighthouse was built there. It also provided a dominant seat for the Frasers of Philorth over their new settlement of Fraserburgh. (Ian Cowe)

fishing industry. As a once proud town was in decline, Kinnaird Head lighthouse, as the centrepiece of the museum, was a beacon for local regeneration and investment. When Sir Alexander built his castle nearly 450 years ago, it is doubtful he could ever have imagined how important, valuable and loved it would become not only to the mariner, but to the people of Fraserburgh.

Kinnaird Head does not have the beauty of Skerryvore or the Isle of May. It has no great mystery like the Flannan Isle, or the scenery and views offered from Ardnamurchan. It is not the Bell Rock. As the exception to the rule, however, its story is the most unique and fascinating of any of the Scottish lighthouses.

Chapter 1

The Castle of Fraserburgh

The history of the castle built on Kinnaird Head is inextricably linked to the formation and proposed development of the town of Fraserburgh and, by virtue of that, it would suffer the same fate as the laird's ambitions. Even before the castle's construction, the Frasers of Philorth, in 1546, had invested heavily in the development of a new harbour for their growing village of Faithlie. Where this investment by Alexander Fraser, the 7th Laird, was canny, calculated and ultimately successful (Faithlie was granted burgh status by 1566), his grandson and successor, Sir Alexander Fraser (*c.* 1537–1623), had greater purpose and ambition for his village of Faithlie, which brought with it heightened financial risks.

The 8th Laird succeeded to his grandfather's estates in 1569, and within a year his significant investments had begun. According to the Fraser family's papers the new laird laid the foundation stone of Kinnaird Head Castle in March 1570. His choice to build on the exposed headland has perplexed many: why would anyone choose to live there when they had use of the mansion of Philorth not five miles away? In all probability this castle was not intended as a full-time residence, but instead built on the headland in order to be seen: it provided a permanent and dominating Fraser presence in the developing settlement. A number of historians have questioned the date of construction for the castle tower with one academic describing it as 'grossly anachronistic for an improving laird' of the 1570s, with further suggestion that it may have been built by the 7th Laird in the 1540s. His grandson, they say, may have only constructed the so-called 'low buildings'. McKean, a key proponent of this argument, may be correct to an extent for the tower was not the height of fashion for its time.

It was a fairly plain tower with baronial flourishes including two roof turrets and a castle parapet composed of 'a good corbel course, with round projecting bartizans at angles, and square ones in the centre.' Even though the style may have been dated, it should be noted that a second castle at Pittulie was undisputedly built by the 8th Laird in the 1590s with many of the same 'antiquated' features as Kinnaird Head, weighing against McKean's dating theory for this particular north-east corner. The castle tower was built on four storeys with the kitchens at ground level, a large dining hall on the first floor, two good bedrooms on the second floor and a roofed compartment on top (said to be for the servants). The low buildings were on two storeys with slated roofs, one extending from the south face of the tower with another second wing of a similar design and size extending from the east side of the tower. Regardless of anything else, it certainly was not a large castle by any standard.

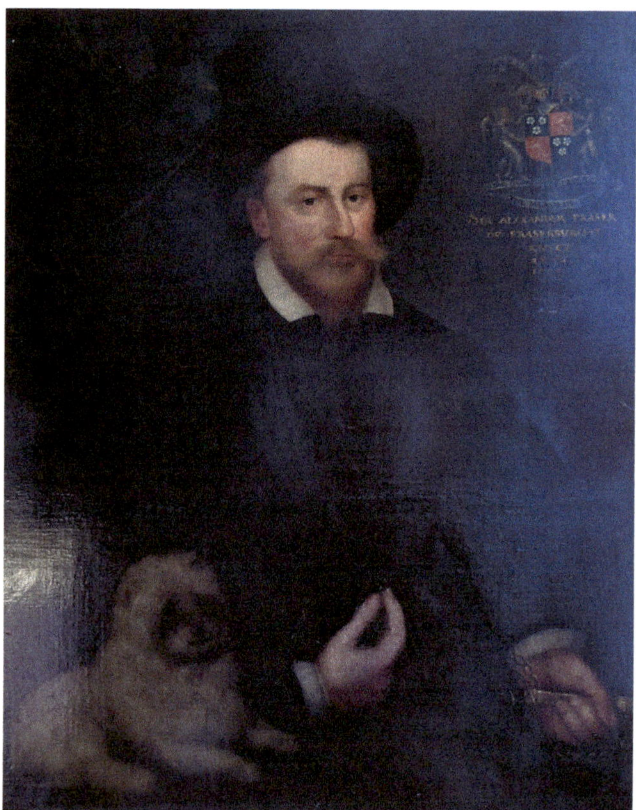

Sir Alexander Fraser, 8th Laird of Philorth *c.* 1537–1623, who built the castle on Kinnaird Head. (Reproduced by kind permission of The Hon. Mrs Nicolson)

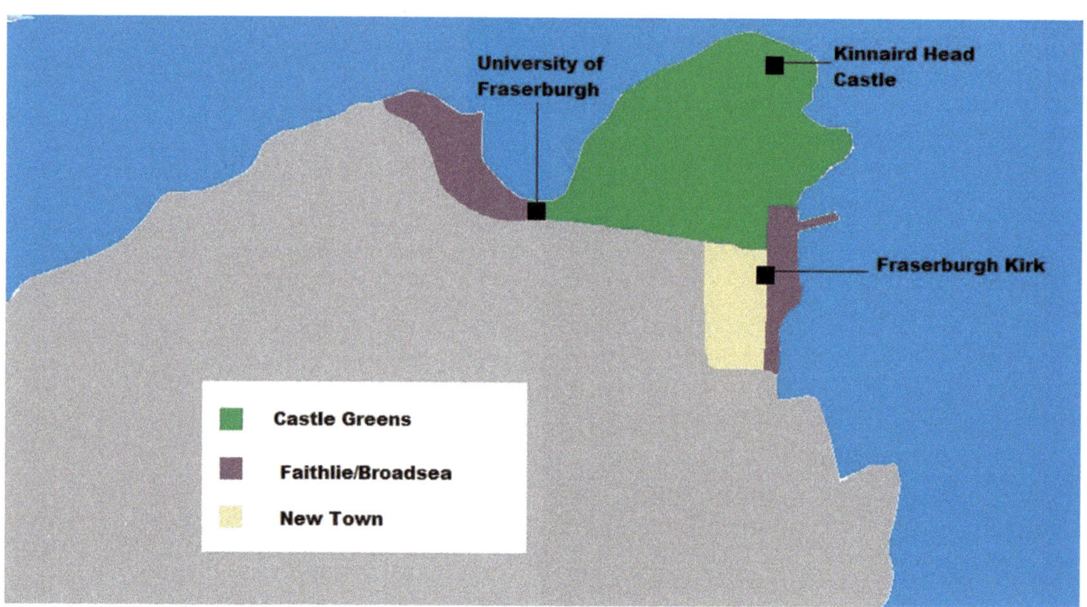

Plan showing the extent of the castle greens in comparison to local settlements. Note the positioning of the church and university.

What has been forgotten to time is that the castle sat in a larger area of empty land referred to as the castle gardens or greens, which isolated the building from the town proper. The effect was to make the castle the centre of Fraser's development with key buildings constructed in alignment to this crowning feature. For example, the boundary of the greens extended as far south to the square where Fraser built the town's new church in 1571. An adherent of the Presbyterian faith, he had it built in the form of a cross and had his own burial aisle constructed on the east of this church, where the old Saltoun Mausoleum now stands. For his boundary on the west he had more ambitious plans: a university.

In 1592 Fraser obtained a charter from James VI that gave him the powers to 'erect and endow' that university. This was further approved by the Scottish Parliament in 1595 and in 1597 Rev Charles Ferme was appointed by the General Assembly to act as both minister of the Parish of Fraserburgh and Principal of the new university. It is known that Sir Alexander went to the expense of constructing a large building for that purpose, all of which has now been removed. In the 1790s Statistical Account, the Rev Alexander Simpson recorded: 'In the west end of the town … is an old quadrangular tower of three storeys, a small part of a large building, intended for a college.' The University of Fraserburgh – Scotland's forgotten university – failed within a decade, something hastened by the Principal's decision to attend the illegal Aberdeen Assembly of 1605, which saw him imprisoned by the King for a number of years.

The failure of the university put strain on Sir Alexander's finances so that by the early seventeenth century he was being harassed by his creditors. In order to pay his

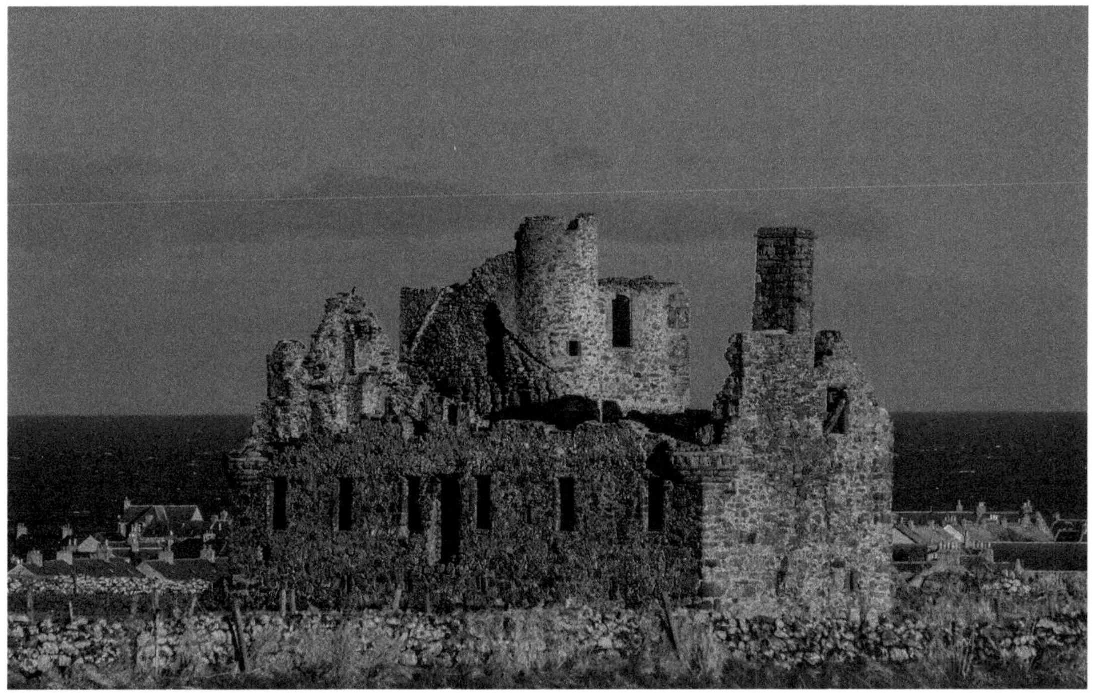

Pitullie Castle, Rosehearty, near Fraserburgh, was built in the 1590s, yet it has much of the outdateed flourishes described by some scholars. (Billy Watson)

debts he sold off swathes of land and property, including the mansion house at Philorth, which forced him to take up full-time residence at Kinnaird Head when in the county. Although his grand plan had ended in failure, it must be noted that by 1601 he had successfully reformed Faithlie into the town of Fraserbugh and had it raised into a burgh of regality. Although his finances were depleted, his new town flourished. In his old age his time was spent in his primary residence of Kinnaird Head Castle, where he died in 1623 aged about eighty-six years.

Seventeenth and Eighteenth Centuries

The purpose of the castle after Sir Alexander is not fully known. It is generally accepted that the castle was virtually abandoned by the Fraser family after the 8th Laird's death. due to its exposed position, seeking more sheltered accommodation in the countryside. Despite this the family were still in financial difficulty, as evidenced by the 9th Laird Alexander Fraser (b. 1570), being an 'inmate' in the Aberdeen Tolbooth (jail) over the period 1625 to 1631 for unpaid debts and broken promises. Their fortunes improved initially under Alexander, the 10th Laird (1604–93), who built the new family seat at Philorth in 1666, which again would have rendered Kinnaird Head obsolete as the

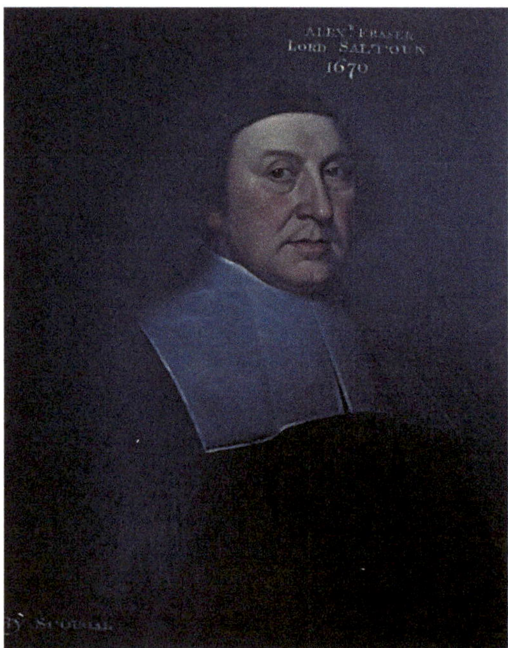

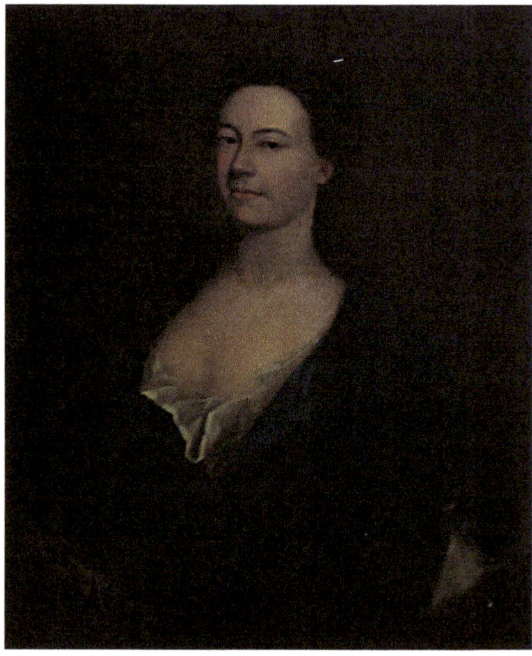

Above left: Alexander, 10th Lord Saltoun (1604–1693), the Covenanting Laird, lived at Kinnaird Head for much of his old age. It should be noted that this title refers to the traditional numbering of the lords, as is preferred by family. (Reproduced by kind permission of The Hon. Mrs Nicolson)

Above right: Margaret Sharp (d. 1734) lived at Kinnaird Head from about 1715 as the Dowager Lady Saltoun. She appears to have been the first dowager to be settled at the castle. (Reproduced by kind permission of The Hon. Mrs Nicolson)

family seat. Known as the 'Covenanting Laird' the 10th Laird fought and invested heavily in the Bishop Wars (1639/40) against the crown, before then fighting for the Royalists in the wars against Cromwell following the unforgivable execution of an anointed king. He was severely wounded at the Battle of Worcester (1651) and it is said he survived and evaded capture only due to his servant pulling him off the battlefield and bolting for the north. In 1669 he inherited the title 10th Lord Saltoun of Abernethy through his mother's line, which gave him a seat in the Scottish Parliament, but also saddled him with the Abernethy family's debts. Like his grandfather, he was forced to resign his estates to his heir and again spent much of his old age in his apartments at Kinnaird Head where he died in August 1694, aged eighty-nine.

In an account from 1721 Kinnaird Head was described as 'the jointure house of the dowager of Saltoun', the Jacobite Cess roll of 1715 confirming that the dowager was living in a Fraserburgh property with relatively high value. It seems that in the eighteenth century the castle had become a standard settlement of widowhood for the dowager Lady Saltoun. In 1715 this was Margaret Sharpe (d. 1734), widow of the 11th Lord Saltoun. She was a daughter to Rev James Sharpe, the infamous Archbishop of St Andrew's, who was murdered by the Covenanters on Magnus Muir. Another dowager, Lady Mary Gordon, died at the castle in February 1753. Becoming a widow in 1748, her son had a new small wing built on the east face of the castle in 1749 for her comfort and privacy.

Privacy would have been required, as it is said that other residents were living in the castle during the period; John Gordon of Kinellar and his wife Henrietta Fraser. They were certainly living in the property by 1731 for the Fraser history recorded that at least one of their daughters, Eleanora, was born there in that year. They were present in the castle following the Jacobite rebellion of 1745 and, despite Lord Saltoun's loyalty to the Hanoverians, were harassed by government forces who were said to carry out searches of the castle. It was noted in the Christian Watt Papers that: 'When Hanoverian troopers searched the castle she [Henrietta] supervised the opening of every drawer and press, and she told them if they stole anything she would have them court martialled.' Her husband John had come out for the 1715 uprising, marching on Aberdeen for James VIII with Earl Marischal. That, and their commitment to episcopacy (she was a daughter of 11th Lord Saltoun and Margaret Sharpe) may have led to their targeting.

Henrietta Fraser died at Kinnaird in 1751, her husband and unmarried daughters residing there until about 1756 when their daughter Eleanora married her cousin George, 14th Lord Saltoun (1720–81). With the bride, the father and his unmarried daughters left Kinnaird Head behind for the Saltoun's seat at Philorth House. With no surviving dowager, the castle was advertised for rent in 1771 as the 'Mansions-house of Kinnaird's head', described as 'large, in good repair, fit for accommodating a large family and also very proper for a merchant.' There is no evidence of any tenant expressing an interest in the residence.

A decade later Eleanora Gordon was widowed and so once again the right to use the castle went to her as dowager. A letter from Lord Saltoun to Eleanora, written in February 1786, describes the castle as 'beginning to go to ruin, and will more and more daily.' He continued to his mother: 'I think I have heard you say so, that if you were to return to live in Aberdeenshire, that you would not live there.' Instead of being resident, Eleanora had at least one weaver employed and living at the castle, Lord Saltoun informing her that even that weaver 'complains that he cannot remain in it,

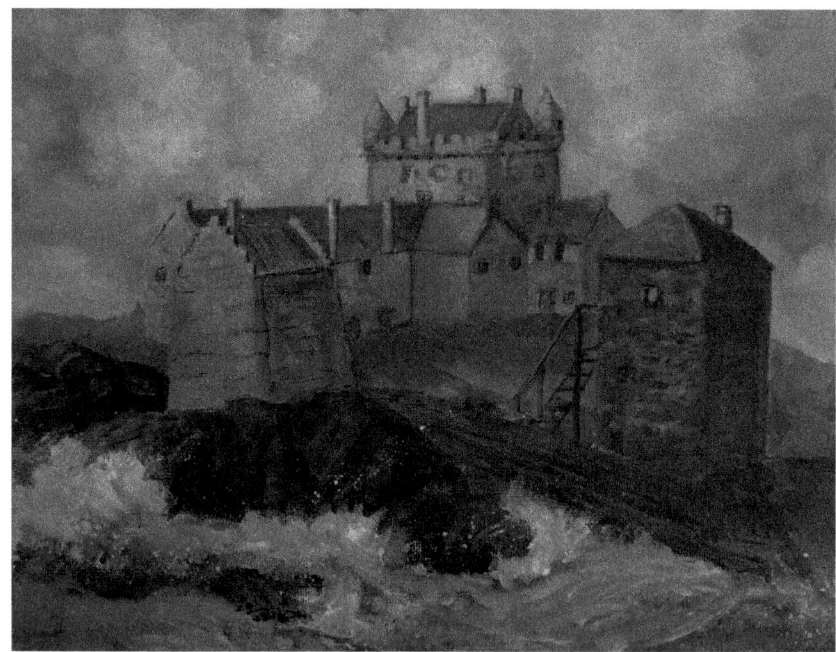

An artist's impression of Kinnaird Head Castle as it would have looked from the south *c.* 1750. (With grateful thanks to Lesley J. Jennings)

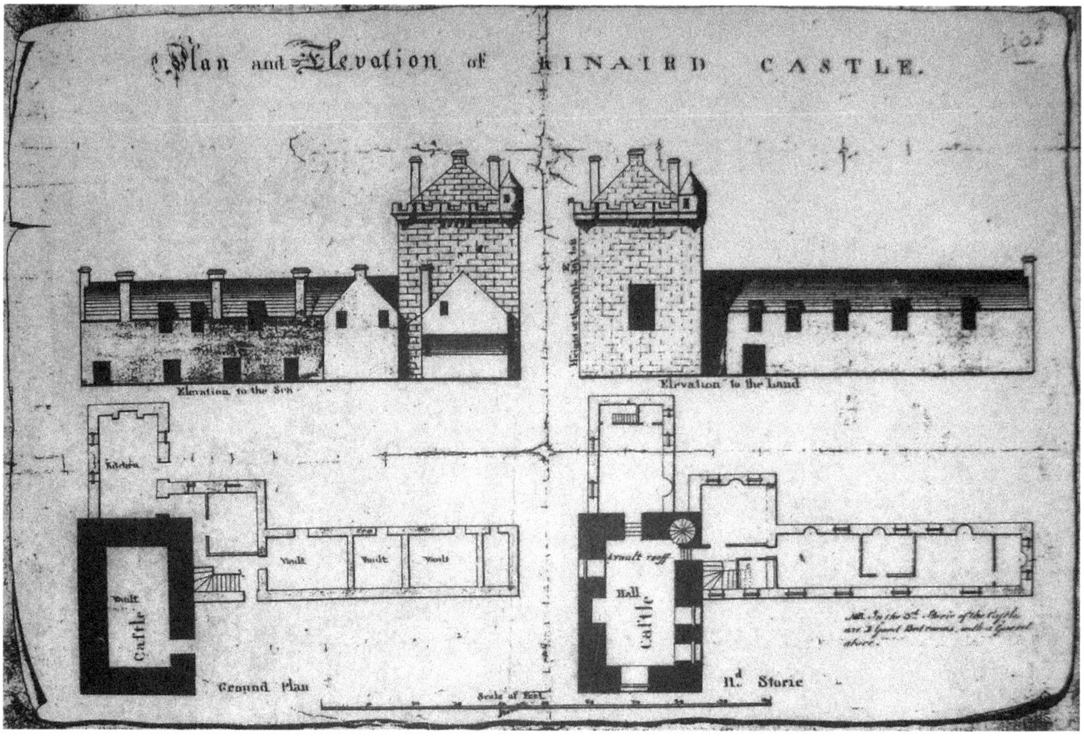

The only contemporary drawing of Kinnaird Head as a castle, 1786. (Original held at National Library of Scotland)

for water drawing.' The presence of weavers at the castle was confirmed in 1861 by eighty-three-year-old weaver John Murison who recalled, 'I have been told that one of the ladies at Philorth employed weavers to weave cloth which was a very common thing in my time – and that they worked in those low buildings which lay east of the castle.'

Thus from 1570 to the dawn of the lighthouse in 1786 the castle had gone from being a symbol of the promise and ambition of Sir Alexander Fraser's vision of Fraserburgh, to a ruin which was not even a fit working environment for eighteenth-century weavers. From a combination of neglect and its exposed position on the coast, the centrepiece of Sir Alexander's planned town was in virtual ruins.

Wine Tower

With the exception of the main tower, the only other castle structure to survive to the present day is the mysterious Wine Tower. It is now a three- (formerly four-) storey tower perched on the sea edge about fifty yards to the south-east of the old castle tower. The bottom floor is accessible only by an exterior hatch, the middle chamber from an internal hatch from the top chamber itself, and the top chamber from an external door accessible by a ladder or stair. Due to its plain structure it could have been built any time between 1400 and 1600, but the common belief is that it was built at about the same time of the castle in 1570.

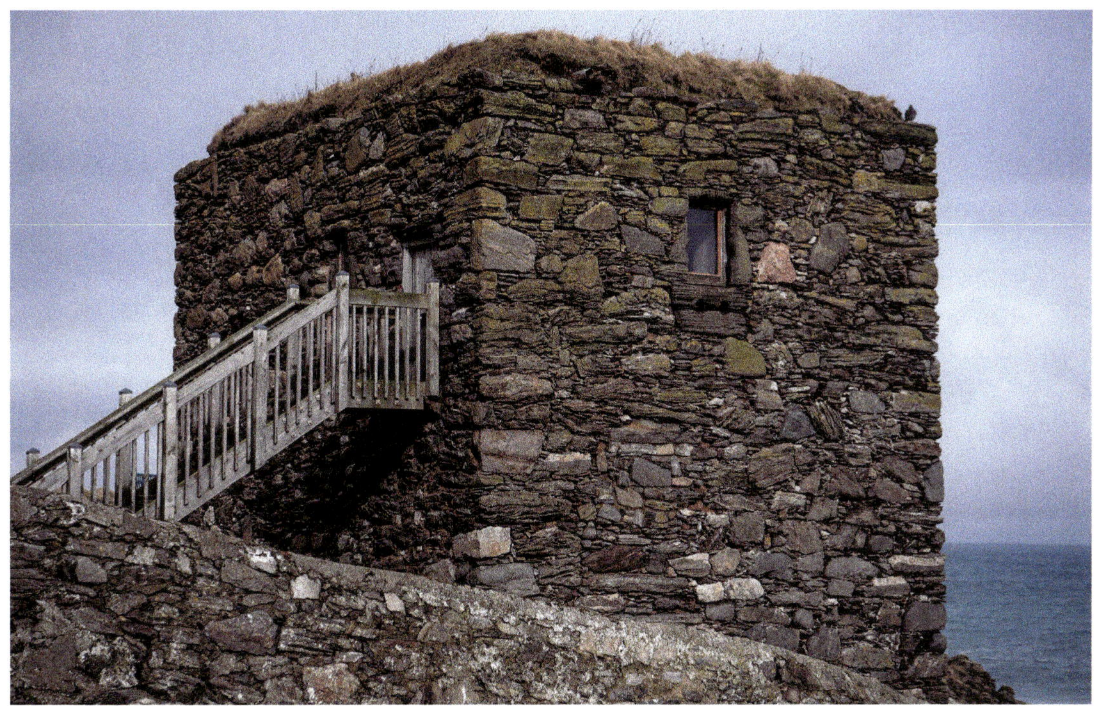

The Wine Tower (or Wynd Tower) is a building steeped in legend and mystery which has baffled scholars for over a century. (Billy Watson)

The mystery of the building stems from the fact that no satisfactory explanation has been accepted for its original purpose. By the 1990s the prevailing argument was that the tower was a secret chapel used by the Frasers post-Reformation. This theory had been widely accepted for much of the twentieth century owing to the existence of carved heraldic stones hanging from the ceiling of the top chamber recognising the church, the king and the Frasers' barony. One, the 'Arma Christi' stone, was composed of the arms of Christ featuring 'instruments of the passion'. 'Chapelists' also pointed to a recess in the north-west of that chamber that they claimed was a priest hole or confessional.

Dr David Murison, a renowned academic who helped compose the *National Dictionary of Scotland*, convincingly deconstructed this theory by pointing out that the chapel chamber was wrongly orientated. Instead of an altar on the east wall there was only a fireplace, suggesting a more domestic purpose. The Arma Christi stone (representing Christ and the Church), he stated, was also commonly used in non-religious structures post-Reformation and at any rate the stones were orientated on a north–south axis, not east to west as would be expected in a chapel. There is little doubt that the Frasers were 'good Protestants', as evidenced by the building of a Presbyterian church and university. Lastly that recess was not a priest hole, but a latrine! Dr Murison convincingly argues that the Wine Tower was simply another domestic part of the castle and, as the name suggests, perhaps one where the drink was stored and flowed freely while the laird was entertaining.

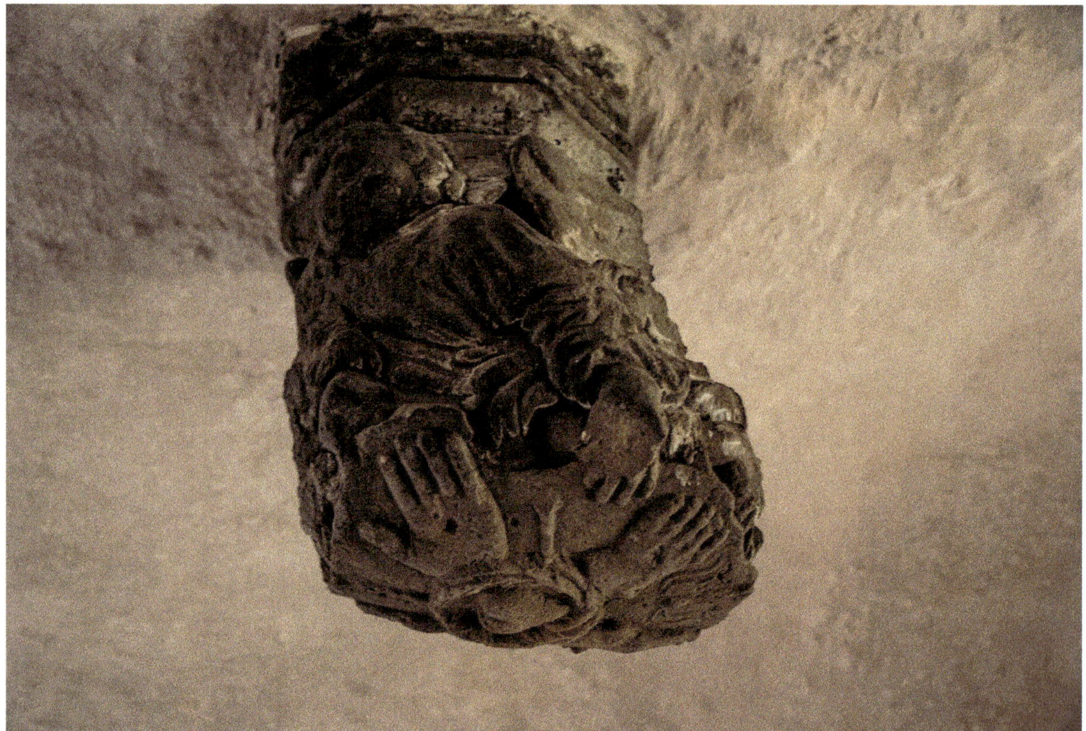

The presence of the 'Arma Christi' stone, with its symbols of the passion, led many to believe that the Wine Tower may have been a secret post-reformation chapel for the Fraser family. (Billy Watson)

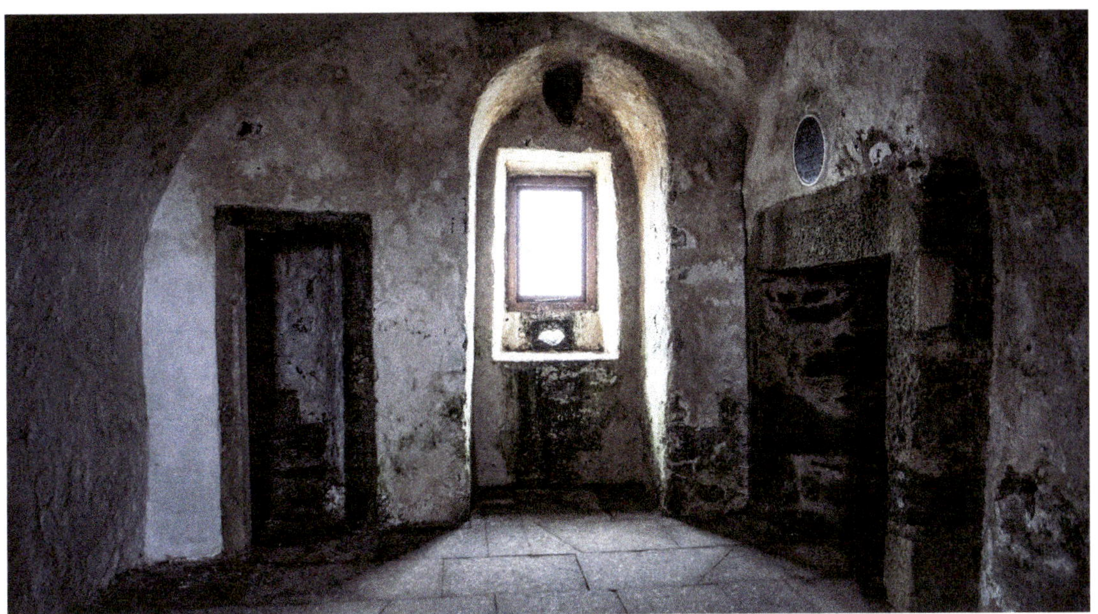

The interior of the upper chamber of the Wine Tower. Dr David Murison argued it had the wrong orientation for a chapel with a fireplace on the east wall – where you would expect an altar – and a latrine recess on the west wall. (Billy Watson)

Its isolated position meant it fell out of use and was left to the elements in the eighteenth century. Its next official purpose came in about 1800 when the Fraserburgh Volunteer force were given permission to use it as an ammunition and powder store in preparation of a Napoleonic invasion. When the threat subsided, the building was again abandoned and it was stated that in 1817 the famous lighthouse engineer, Robert Stevenson, wanted to convert it into an oil store for the lighthouse. He was advised by training keeper John Reid that the building was the property of Lord Saltoun and the matter went no further. The volunteers, being reformed in 1859, were again given permission to use the building as a magazine and altered it for that purpose but the commissioners of Northern Lighthouses were unsure. They claimed the building was their property and objected to it being used to store explosives so close to their light. The matter came to a head in 1864 when the commissioners engaged in legal action against Lord Saltoun who, having no inclination to engage in such an insignificant case, agreed to cede ownership to the commissioners on the express understanding that they were not to demolish or alter the building in any way, so that it may stand 'as an ornament' to the town. It is likely thanks to that agreement that the Wine Tower stands today.

Chapter 2

Scotland's Leading Light

In 1782 an almost unprecedented series of storms caused havoc with shipping, leading to many vessels being lost to the seas around Scotland. This storm focussed the attention of the government; for as long as the Scottish coast remained untamed, the wealth of the nation would continue to be lost to the seabed. Kinnaird Head had long been viewed as an ideal point on which to erect a lighthouse, a 1785 account of Fraserburgh stating, 'It has been always thought by mariners, that a light-house erected there would tend materially to the preservation engaged in commerce upon the coast... seldom a winter passes, says Captain Kyd, without shipwrecks.'

Alexander Fraser, 15th Lord Saltoun, saw an opportunity for his crumbling castle as in late 1785 he met with Captain James Kydd to discuss the establishment of a

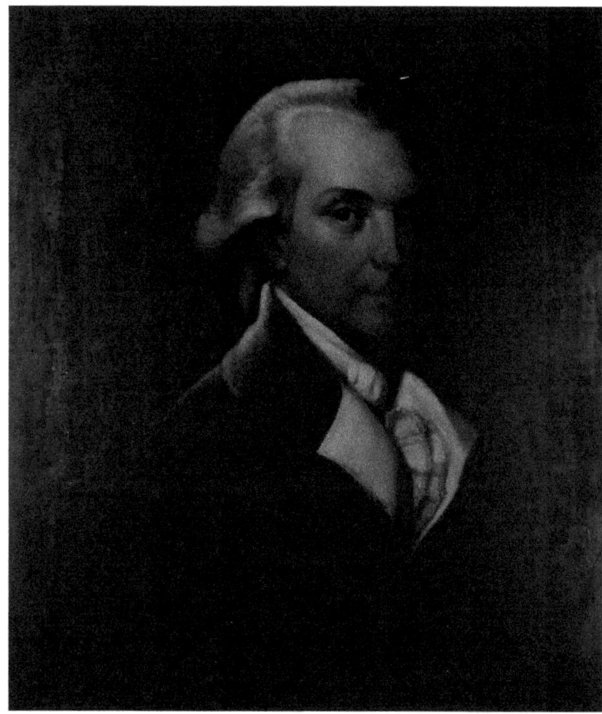

Alexander, 15th Lord Saltoun 1758–93, initially had plans to build a private lighthouse before negotiating a lease for the castle with the Northern Lighthouse Trustees. (Reproduced by kind permission of The Hon. Mrs Nicolson)

lighthouse at Kinnaird Head. In a subsequent letter to Lord Saltoun in December 1785, Kydd explains the mechanics of how private lighthouses were funded: 'There must be a tax on the Tonnage of Shipping voted by Parliament for its support', further advising Lord Saltoun to make his application to Parliament as 'soon as possible' while the mood was favourable. He assured Lord Saltoun that both he and his friend Captain Brown would give favourable testimony in the Parliamentary Committees when their opinions were sought. Saltoun's interest was clear: he wanted to cut his losses on the ruinous Kinnaird Head Castle and convert it into a private lighthouse from which he could collect all shipping dues for his estate's enrichment. This was the true purpose of his letter to his mother in February 1786, discussed in the previous chapter – to ensure that she would give up her settlement right to the property without issue. His letter stated: 'My wish would be to keep up the Old Tower watertight, in the event of obtaining the establishment of a Lighthouse thereon, which would be very advantageous to the Shipping on this Coast, and beneficial for the Estate.'

Northern Lighthouse Board

Unfortunately for Lord Saltoun his plan for a private lighthouse was scuppered by the efforts of George Dempster (1732–1818), Member of Parliament for the Fife and Forfar Burghs, who pushed for the Bill that would create the Northern Lighthouse Board (NLB). Much of the proposals Dempster pushed through the committees were drafted into the final Bill that passed through Parliament – with no objections – on 27 June 1786. The Act for Erecting Certain Lighthouses in the Northern Parts of Great Britain created the first organisation in the world that had been established solely for the purpose of building and managing lighthouses on a nationwide basis. Furthermore, the Act set out where these first four lights would be built: Eilean Glas; Mull of Kintyre; North Ronaldsay; and Kinnaird Head. It seems Kydd and Brown's voices had been heard by the committees after all!

There was, perhaps, one issue: the trustees, composed of two Crown Officers of Scotland and seventeen other lord provosts, provosts, baillies and sheriffs of regions on the coast, had next to no knowledge of how to build or manage a lighthouse. It is doubtful that any of them had even set foot in a lighthouse. At their first meeting in Edinburgh on 1 August it is little surprise that most of their time was spent in gathering information and seeking advice 'relative to the best construction of Lighthouses and other particulars relative to them'. The Board was tasked not only with building the lights but also in acquiring the land, and all this would need to be achieved with no more than £1,200.

It was at this first meeting that the trustees first met Thomas Smith, a tinsmith and lamp-maker from Edinburgh, who presented them with a model of a lighthouse parabolic reflector. Smith was by no means the inventor of the parabolic reflector but it seems he was the first to make one in Scotland. They had first been designed in England in 1763 by William Hutchinson but were not widely in use. At their second meeting, the trustees were advised to contact Ezekiel Walker (1741–1834) of Kings Lynn who had built and used his own design of reflectors at the Hunstanton lighthouse, Norfolk, in 1778. The trustees approached him to find 'whether he would choose to undertake the erection of them [their lighthouses] or oversee the execution.' The proposal was

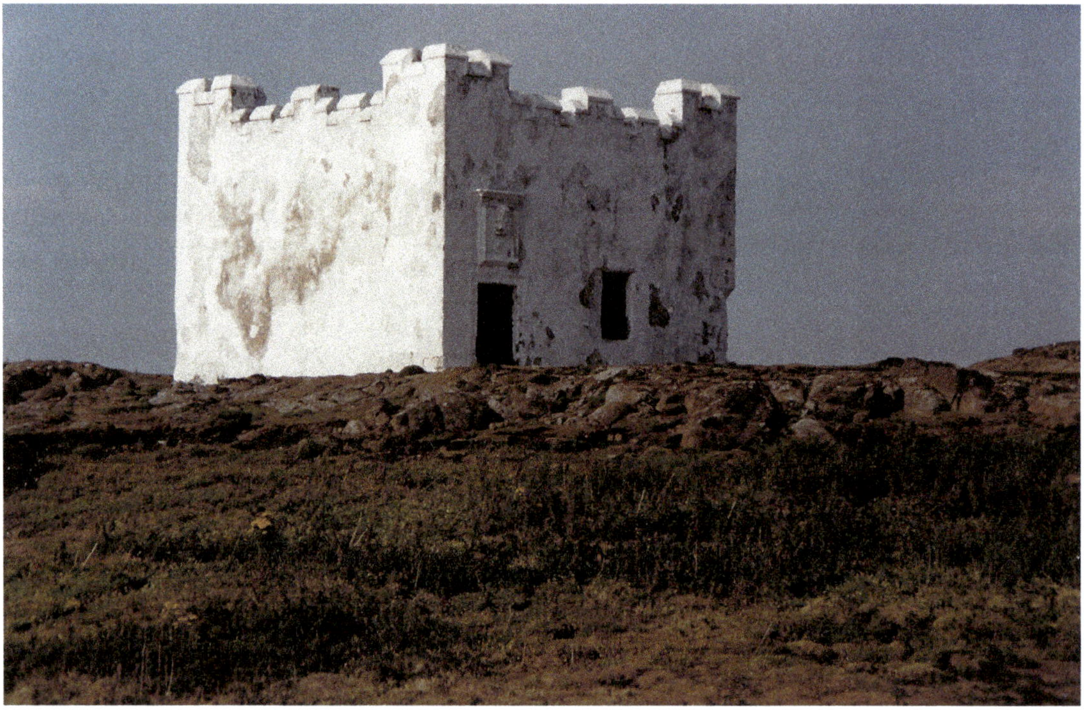

Before the establishment of the Northern Lighthouse Board, the Isle of May beacon, a private lighthouse lit by coals in a brazier, was the best navigational aid in Scotland. Unfortunately in adverse weather the open coals were often extinguished. (Collection of the Museum of Scottish Lighthouses, Fraserburgh)

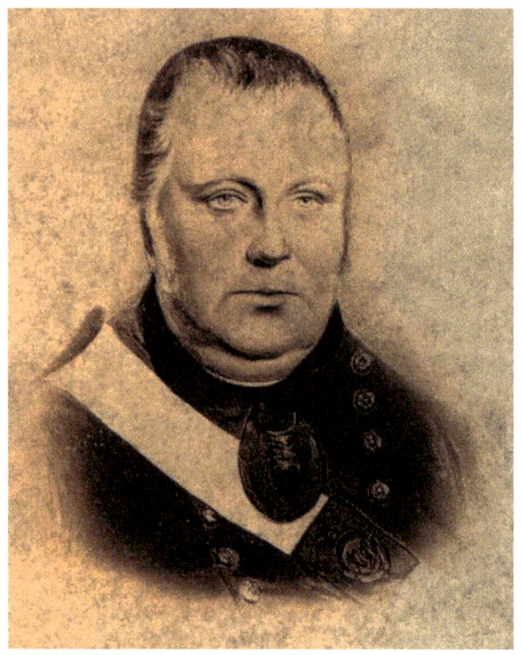

The Trustees of Northern Lights were first encouraged to approach Ezekiel Walker, an English Lighthouse builder and scientist, to build their first four lights. (With thanks to the descendants of Ezekiel Walker)

ultimately rejected by Walker who instead offered 'that he would come here and erect one of the lighthouses himself and give directions for the other three for fifty Guineas and instruct any person the trustees thought proper.'

The trustees had been impressed with Thomas Smith's 'proposals for constructing the lighthouses by lamps and reflectors', but initially rejected his service 'on account of his want of experience'. The offer from Walker gave Smith a lifeline, the trustees sending him to Norfolk to be instructed in how to make and manage parabolic reflectors, but also in the building of the towers. Astonishingly, Smith's apprenticeship as a lighthouse engineer was over by 21 March 1787 – after a period of about two months. He was later appointed the first Engineer of the Northern Lighthouse Board while, despite his critical role, Walker has regrettably become almost forgotten to the history of Scottish lighthouses.

In addition to securing a competent engineer to build their lights, the trustees were at the same time engaged in negotiations to acquire the land they required for building the lights. Negotiations began with Lord Saltoun by letter on 26 September 1786 to acquire 'so much land as may be necessary and to erect proper lighthouses with such other

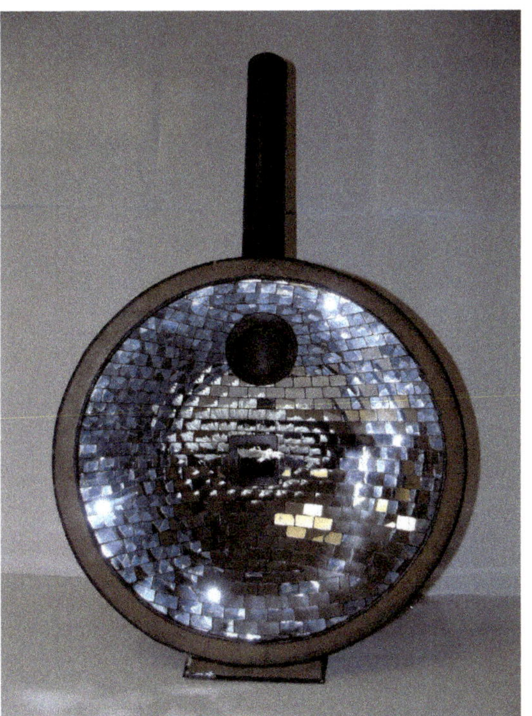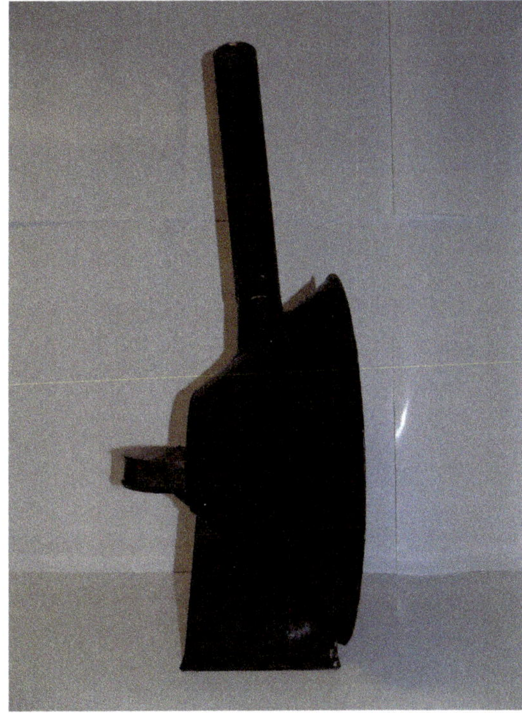

Above left: An example of a parabolic reflector: a whale oil lamp was set into the centre of the reflector so that when the wicks were lit, the flame would be reflected on the many squares of mirrored glass on the parabolic curve. (Collection of the Museum of Scottish Lighthouses, Fraserburgh)

Above right: The profile of a parabolic reflector showing the argand-style chimney to allow the smoke to escape. Whale oil gave off a great deal of soot requiring the keepers to wipe down the reflectors regularly. (Collection of the Museum of Scottish Lighthouses, Fraserburgh)

buildings conveniences as to them shall appear necessary and also to erect harbours or wharfs for landing coals … for burning'. Saltoun replied a month later sending a plan of the grounds and the castle tower to the trustees along with a price for his property, which was more than they could afford. They replied to His Lordship on 16 January emphasising 'the Act of Parliament allows the trustees to expend only to the extent of £1,000, for building all four of the Light Houses … in these circumstances your Lordship sees it is impossible for the trustees to think of purchasing at the value mentioned in your Lordship's letter … the value far exceeds any sum the trustees can afford to give.' Acquiring the castle would be too expensive, and so the trustees proposed that they would purchase a piece of land to the east of the castle with the intention of building a new tower for their purposes.

The issue was resolved on 30 March at the trustees' fifth official meeting where Lord Saltoun himself was in attendance to negotiate the transfer of his land. He clearly persuaded the trustees of the value of the castle 'and the saving they would make by erecting the lighthouse on top of the castle'. Rather than sell the castle, Lord Saltoun agreed a perpetual feu (rent) for the castle and 1½ acres in favour of the trustees. The feu duty was set at only seven pounds sterling to be paid annually starting Marinmas (11 November) 1787. Why Lord Saltoun changed his mind on the value of his property is unknown. Perhaps he saw the public good of a lighthouse on his lands, as well as the potential growth it could encourage in his port. Alternatively, as he suggested to his own mother just a year earlier, disposing of his almost ruinous castle was a saving in itself as at least now it would be no burden on his estate. It was a deal which suited both parties.

The First Lighthouse

The trustees were eager to get a start on their lighthouses, not least because they would be unable to collect lighting dues – and therefore have no income – until all four of their lights were constructed. Thomas Smith was dispatched to Fraserburgh in late April 1787 'in view of employing workmen to erect the building … and dispose of the roof and any other part of the building which will not be required'. Lord Saltoun proved most useful to the works, allowing his own mason to be employed in the construction as well as offering advice 'in the execution of a work of so great public utility'. Over the summer months the castle of Kinnaird Head was partly demolished with the removal of the roof apartments, parapet towers and some of the low buildings. The roof was further fireproofed using lead sheets in preparation for the arrival of Smith's lantern, which was under construction in Edinburgh along with Smith's parabolic reflectors.

There are not many descriptions of Smith's lantern other than that the main body of it was made of timber, which held square window panes. The floor and the lantern top were both constructed of metal in an attempt to fireproof the most vulnerable parts of the lantern. The lantern was presented to the trustees 'and a variety of other persons' in late August, before it was again dismantled and loaded aboard the lighthouse ship for delivery in Fraserburgh. At their meeting on 30 August, it was 'resolved that the lantern to be erected at Kinnaird's head be lighted as soon as ready'. At this same meeting the trustees turned their attention to recruiting a lightkeeper, leaving this selection to the engineer who was also to instruct his nominated keeper. The lantern was built and re-glazed during September and the parabolic reflectors – which sailed north with the

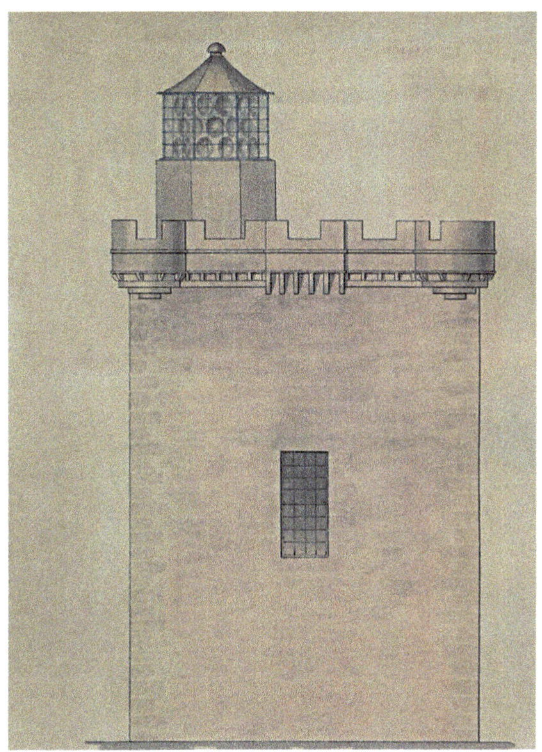

A later plan by Alan Stevenson, showing Thomas Smith's lantern on Kinnaird Head Castle. Note the arrangement of the reflectors in the lantern.

lantern – were set in their place. The reflectors – seventeen in total – were arranged on shelves at three levels: six each on the top and bottom shelves, with five on the middle shelf. They were purposely staggered out of vertical alignment so that the five on the middle shelf better filled the gaps between those on the top and bottom shelves, thus ensuring that there were limited dull spots in the array.

On 16 November it was reported that the lighthouse at Kinnaird Head was now complete and that it would be lighted for the first time on 1 December 1787. At the same meeting Smith announced he had chosen James Park, Shipmaster, 'as a proper person to take care of the lighthouse'. Interestingly it seems Smith sought advice locally to find Mr Park, as it was noted in the Board minutes that the original recommendation came from 'Lord Saltoun and certification from a number of other persons'. For being Scotland's first NLB keeper, little is known about Park other than his previous employment as a shipmaster and that he was said to be about seventy years of age when he was appointed keeper. It was further decided that he would be employed 'during pleasure at one shilling the night with benefit of some ground on condition that he has another person with him every night who he is to instruct'. He was also provided with accommodation, this being principally the 'new' wing of the castle low buildings erected in 1749. Park was given a list of seven lengthy instructions on how to maintain the light, the main duty being to 'light that lamp half an hour after Sun-setting and keep them burning till half an hour before Sunrising everyday for which purpose you must attend them every two or three hours throughout the night' which he did for the first time, as published, on 1 December 1787.

The effect of the light was praised by seafarers with newspapers keen to print their observations on the new lighthouse. Captain Bain passed the light on 12 December noting that he 'saw it distinctly at five leagues (seventeen miles), at all different points' and further that it was quite steady making it 'superior in that respect to the light of May'. Allan McKenzie of Stornoway gave his opinion: 'I think it will be superior to any light on the coast, and equal to any I ever saw.' A later correspondent in February 1788 reported that the light was 'seen at ten leagues distance, like a faint star'. Using Smith's reflectors, and following Ezekiel Walker's direction, the trustees had created one of the most brilliant and powerful lights of its time: no mean feat considering this was the organisation's first light. Kinnaird Head was Scotland's leading light and from this lone light in the darkness – built on top of a castle – the Northern Lighthouse Board would quickly rise to become a revered and respected institution.

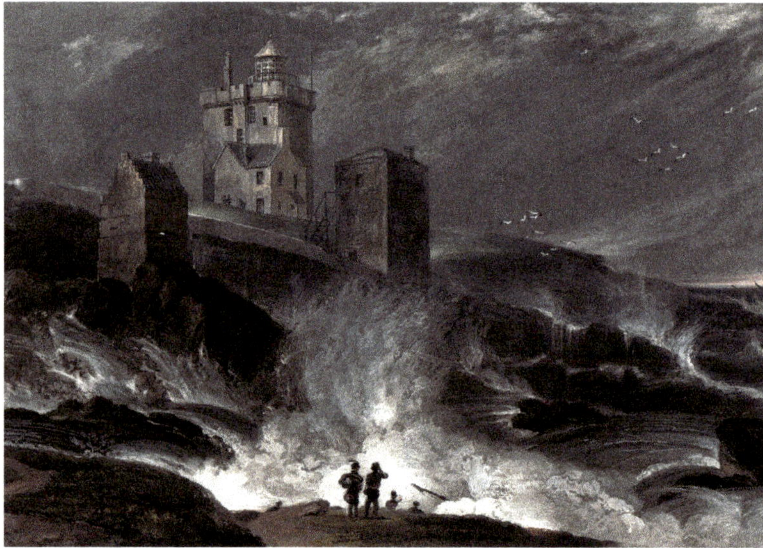

Kinnaird Head Lighthouse in 1821/22, showing Thomas Smith's lantern. The keepers lived in the remaining castle low buildings rent free. (William Daniell, 1822)

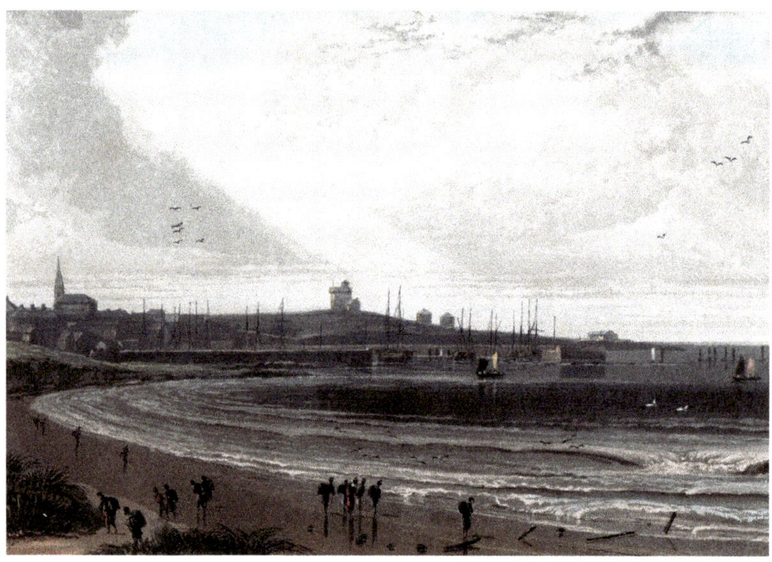

Even into the 1820s the castle remained apart from the town of Fraserburgh, with the majority of the old castle greens still being owned by the Fraser family estate. (William Daniell, 1822)

Chapter 3

National Establishment

The trustees' first four lights were undoubtedly effective and brought high praise from mariners but it would be a fair judgement to say the construction standard of the masonry of the towers were neither as professional or advanced as the lights under Trinity House. Indeed, this is not surprising given the inexperience of the first Engineer to the Board who was principally a tinsmith and lamp-maker. Despite the appearance of the first towers, their lights were powerful and demand for more quickly followed in Scotland, so that by 1794 the trustees had built two additional lights at Pladda and Pentland Skerries. The Skerries light was the first at which Robert Stevenson (1772–1850), step-son and apprentice to Thomas Smith, played a leading role superintending the works. Robert was to go on to serve as Engineer to the Board jointly

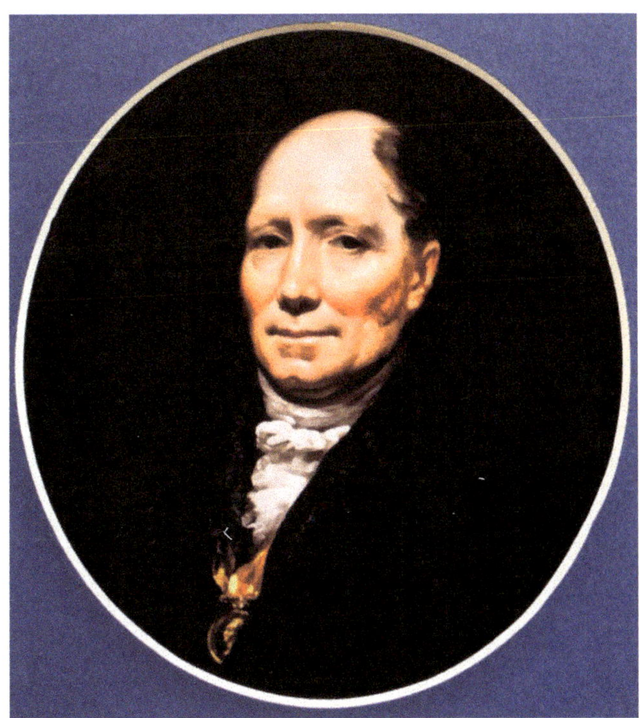

Robert Stevenson (1772–1850), succeeded his step-father Thomas Smith as Engineer to the Northern Lighthouse Board.

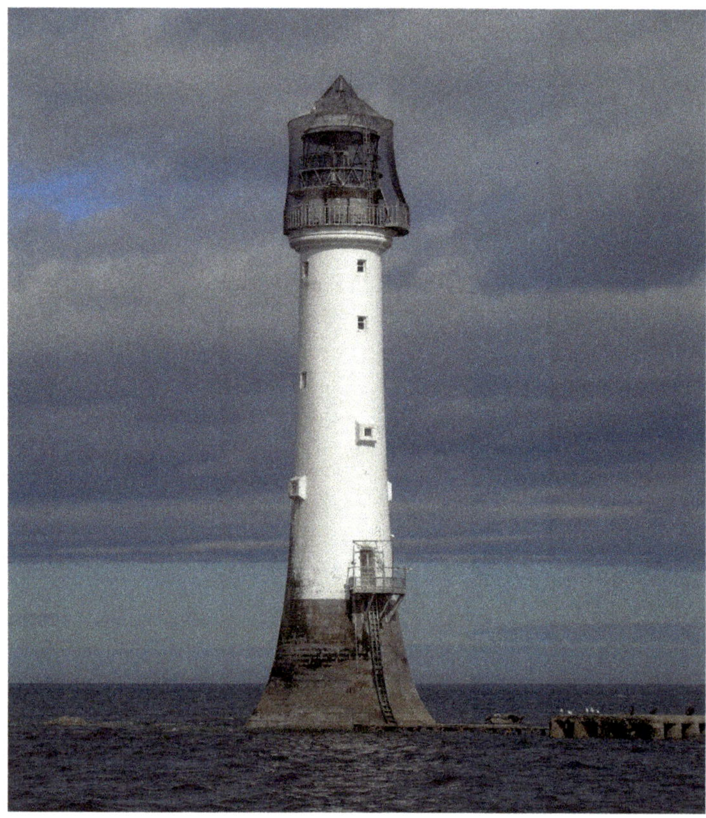

The Bell Rock Lighthouse was Robert's – and the Stevenson family's – crowning achievement.

with Smith from 1797, serving as sole engineer from 1808 up to his own retirement in 1842. It was the building of the Bell Rock lighthouse (1807–11) that made his and his family's name, in the process marking the maturity of the Northern Lighthouse Board as a lighthouse authority equal to any other in the world.

Light-keeping

Although Robert is perhaps most famed for his work as a lighthouse builder and engineer, it was his influence more than any other which shaped the NLB and changed light-keeping into a professional occupation in Scotland. A strict but fair official, Robert was to write most of the rules and set the standard of light-keeping and, as this chapter will later show, through his paternalistic outlook, would see that his keepers were provided for in old age. As noted, Robert became the joint engineer to the Board in early 1797, months before James Park, Kinnaird Head and Scotland's first NLB keeper, resigned his post 'having informed of his being unable to do his duty as keeper of Kinnaird Lighthouse'. After a decade of service he was now about eighty years of age and unable to work. For his service the Board granted him a £5 annuity which was to be taken from the now £30 annual salary of the replacement keeper.

In many respects, after ten years nothing had changed in the Board's recruitment process. Although the post was now salaried, rather than the shilling per night arrangement, new keepers still had no great experience or knowledge of light-keeping bar their initial instruction by the engineer, after which they would be left in the sole charge of the lighthouse. Park's replacement – George Gray – was a mariner from Leith with a wife and young family and although considerably younger than Park, he was already forty-seven years old when he embarked on this new career. He proved to be a diligent keeper as Stevenson noted during his 1798 inspection voyage: 'I found the keeper George Gray now in office six months very attentive to his charge – the lamps very well trimmed, the Reflectors, windows and lantern in general clean.'

During his visit in 1804, however, Stevenson found the lighthouse in a less acceptable condition: 'The lantern was not in so cleanly a state as usual which the keeper said was owing to his want of health when the charge devolved chiefly on his wife who also had at the same time here [a] small family to manage.' In essence, Scotland's lighthouses were family run – a system which Robert would later report to be imperfect. First, in the case of illness it meant there was no qualified person at the station to step in and, secondly, Robert believed ill-discipline was rife at family-run lighthouses for want of a third party. It was not in a wife's interest to report her husband's idleness for she and her children would also lose their income and home. To counter this, from 1815, Robert introduced a system of two keepers to the lighthouse service meaning every light would now have a principal and an assistant keeper. As Robert noted of this new system: 'The two keepers, agreeing ill, will keep one another to their duty.'

A Lighthouse Inside a Castle

As part of his 'National Establishment' works Robert turned his attention to the first lights built 'on the smallest, plainest and most simple plan that could be devised' by the commissioners. Of the first four of these lights, North Ronaldsay had been abandoned in 1809, being made redundant by Robert's flashing light at Start Point; Smith's lantern at Mull of Kintyre was pulled down in 1824 after being replaced by a more substantial tower; and the old lantern at Eilean Glas had been dwarfed by Stevenson's new tower, also built in 1824. With regards to Kinnaird Head, perhaps the most primitive arrangement of all, it very nearly became the first light to be rebuilt in a new location, like at North Ronaldsay. In 1798 petitioners complained that the light did nothing to warn of the great danger of the Rattray Briggs, some 12 miles south of Kinnaird. The petition called for the lantern at Kinnaird to be removed and replaced at Rattray. These complaints were persistent and taken so seriously that in January 1801 the commissioners 'directed the engineer to consider the proposal of removing the lighthouse from Kinnairdshead and erecting one at Rattray Briggs.'

Stevenson duly carried out his survey of the coast as instructed, concluding that while the Kinnaird headland remained the best situation for a light, 'it would be most advisable to erect a new lighthouse at Kinnairdhead, about 100 yards more to the eastward than the castle stands.' It has been suggested by some sources that he contemplated demolishing the castle entirely to make way for the proposed purpose-built lighthouse. He must have thought better of the idea, perhaps thanks to the comments of his friend Sir Walter Scott, who mused in 1814: 'The old castle, now bearing the light, is a picturesque object from the sea.' Stevenson would finally be forced to act on improvements due to the decrepit state of the tower by 1820. In September of that year he noted that the parapet of the castle wall was 'found to be in so frail and shattered a state as to be quite unsafe.' He further noted to the commissioners in 1822 that the roof of the castle 'was some years ago described to be in so hazardous state from the decay of timber of the roof', as well as the rotting away of the timber parts of the lantern due to condensation running down the window panes caused both by the heat from the lamps and the heat from the house below.

Stevenson submitted his plans for the repairs of the lighthouse to the commissioners in January 1822, finally gaining approval to execute his plan in March of that year. The plans were ambitious. Rather than destroy the old castle, he opted to retain it and build a new lighthouse tower through the interior of the existing tower. The plan of works, which has not survived, was drawn up by Robert as engineer but as he was now far too busy to oversee the day-to-day works himself he entrusted the management of the project to his Foreman of Works, Robert Selkirk (1779–1846). Selkirk had been in the

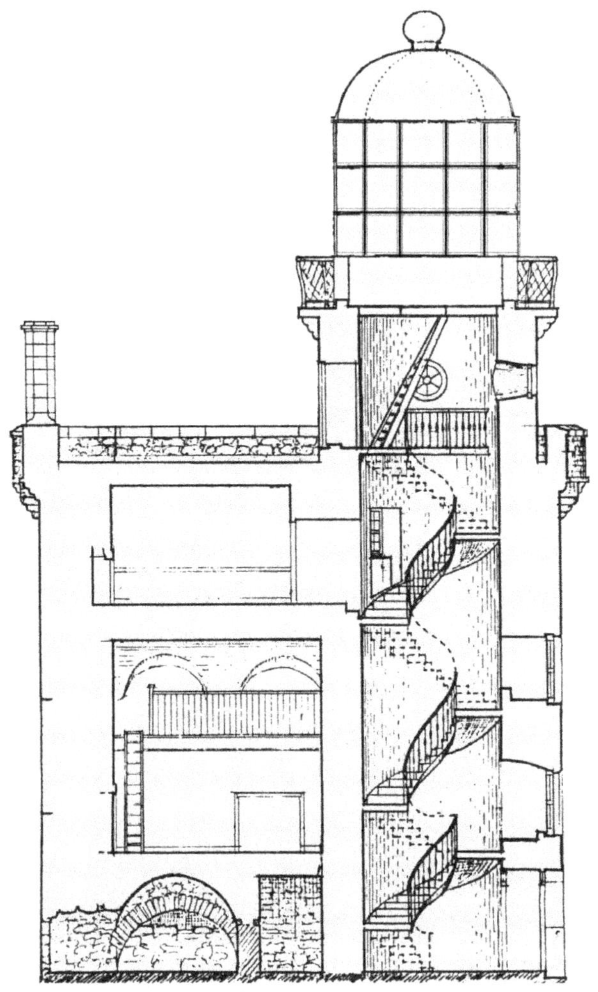

Rather than demolish the castle Stevenson planned to build a new lighthouse tower up through the middle of the castle. (Northern Lighthouse Board)

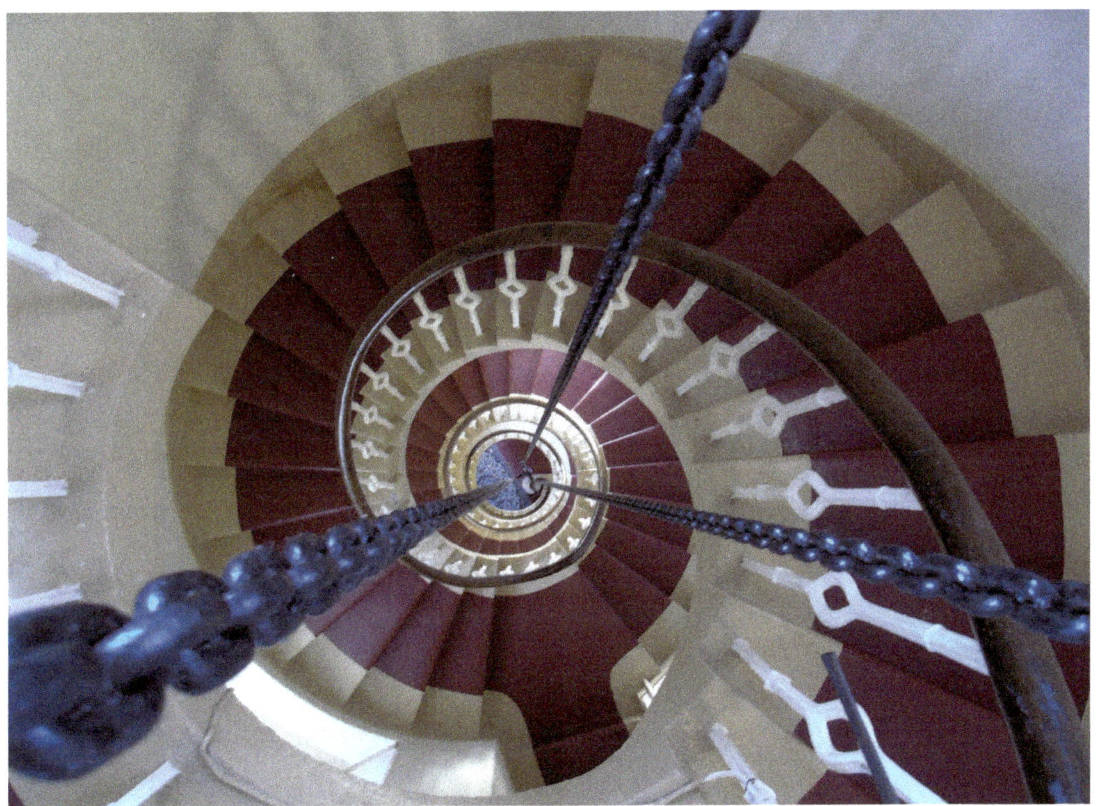

The interior of Robert Stevenson's tower. Although designed by Stevenson, the tower was built on a day-to-day basis by his foreman Robert Selkirk, who was principal builder at the Bell Rock 1808–11.

service of Stevenson since the building of the Bell Rock lighthouse where he served as principal builder, succeeding to that role only after his predecessor, Mr Wishart, met with a serious accident. From 1808 to the end of building Selkirk was responsible for laying every stone of the Bell Rock in place. The works at Kinnaird began in May 1822, with Stevenson directing Selkirk to send him monthly reports outlining the progress of the new tower. Despite this, Stevenson was still a frequent visitor to the site and corresponded regularly with his foreman.

From the letters Stevenson and Selkirk sent to each another we are able to piece together part of the building process. During the first season of building the interior of the old castle was dramatically altered with internal walls and parts of ceilings pulled down to make way for the rise of the new lighthouse tower. Astonishingly, while these works were underway the light was still exhibited as normal during the night but not without causing Mr Gray considerable inconvenience. His oil stores were being affected by the lime dust flying about the place, which was 'most injurious to oil' causing him to move his supplies away from the station. The stones were procured from local quarries and delivered to the site where they were hewed ready for building. The works of the first year ended in early October, Stevenson later reporting to the Board that 'some progress has been made in the works of masonry for supporting the New Lightroom'.

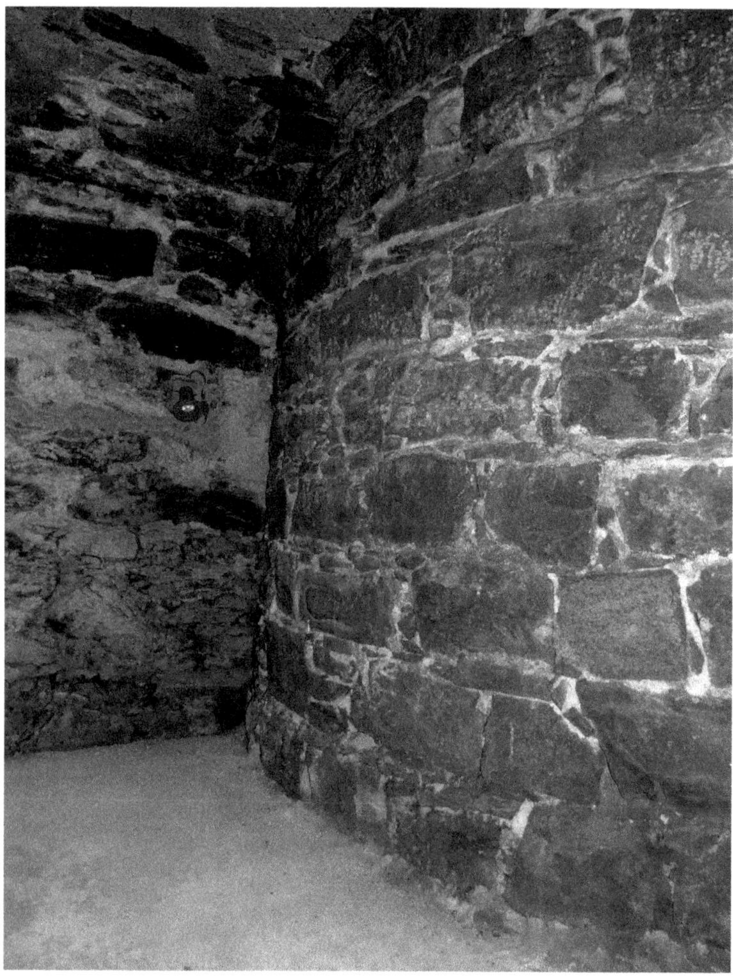

The bottom courses of the new tower, cut and laid in 1822, are still visible in the lighthouse coal store.

The bottom courses of the tower were constructed from rough block stone which did not require to be dressed to any high standard because it was contained within the castle walls and eventually plastered in the interior. As the tower rose higher temporary doors were knocked through the castle walls to allow the stones to be winched up to wooden platforms at higher levels for easier access. These temporary doors would later be converted into three windows, while the last was blocked up with masonry.

It is probable that a substantial portion of the tower was built in the first season as by 23 May 1823, the second season, Selkirk informs Stevenson that the works were so well advanced that they were already ready to remove Thomas Smith's lantern to allow for the new tower to extend through the castle roof. The new lantern would be elevated above the same spot as the old. By the time Smith's lantern was dismantled in June, temporary lights were already in place on the castle roof to ensure there would be no break in the keepers' nightly vigil.

Interesting, the temporary lights sent by Stevenson were 'the lanterns formerly in use on board the Bell Rock Floating Light'. The lightvessel, which served 1807–11, had three lanterns set on masts each of which contained ten small lamps backed with

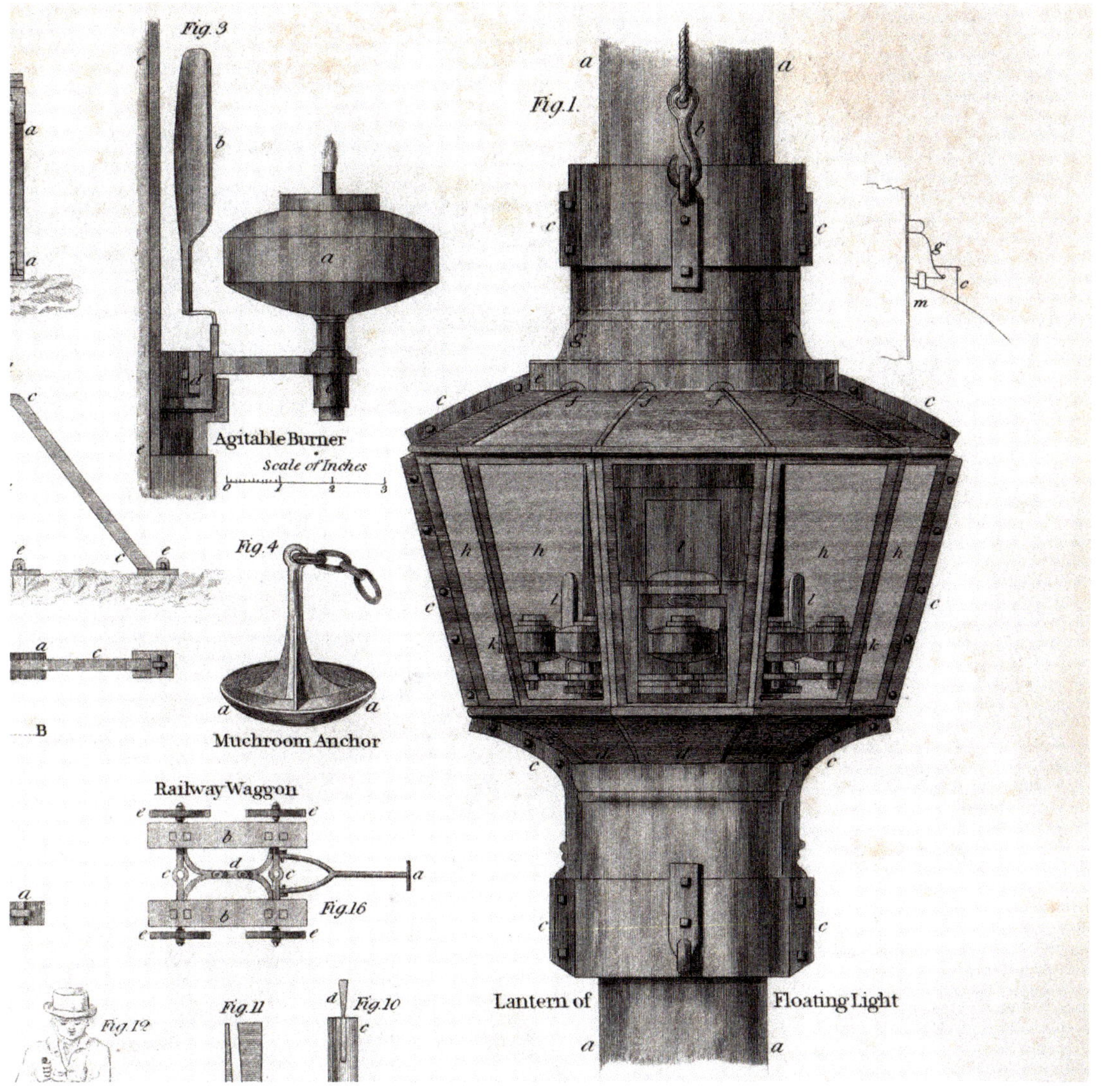

In the late summer of 1823 Kinnaird Head was lit using the temporary lanterns originally used to mark the Bell Rock reef by the lightvessel *Pharos* during the construction of the famous lighthouse between 1807 and 1811. (Stevenson's Account of the Building of Bell Rock Lighthouse)

silver-plated reflectors. Like the setup on the actual vessel it can be presumed these lamps were elevated on masts to raise them to a similar height of the former lantern. The complexity of the lamps, and perhaps the age of both serving keepers at Kinnaird, prompted Stevenson to send two new assistants to serve under Mr Gray, while his former assistant 'was sent to Inchkeith where the duty is more easy.'

The building work appeared to slow in the summer of 1823, perhaps due to the additional labour in hewing and dressing the visible granite sections of the tower. It also seems that that there was a hold-up for want of granite on the site, requiring more to be ordered from a Mr Couper's quarry to finish the tower's 'plinth or upper leaf of cornice'.

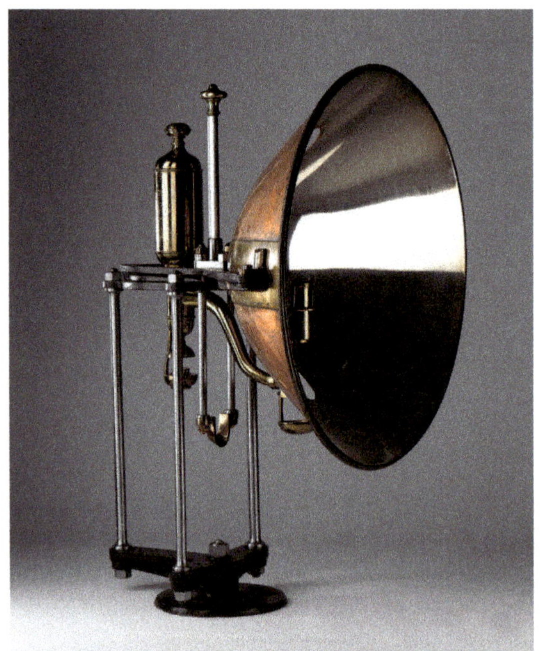 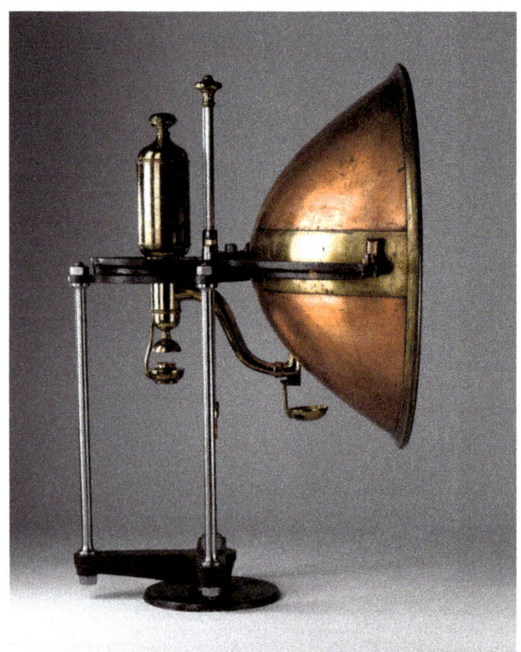

Above left: Robert Stevenson's improved design of the parabolic reflector was composed of a copper bowl with a silvered face for reflection. It is not known how many reflectors were used at Kinnaird, but there were likely twenty-one – the same number there had been since 1793. (© National Museum of Scotland)

Above right: The new reflectors had more advanced oil canisters behind the bowl that could be heated in the winter months to allow the oil to burn more smoothly. (© National Museum of Scotland)

The work was beginning to slide behind schedule with Stevenson telling his foreman on 4 August that he hoped his squad of men would soon be reduced in number, while a month later Selkirk received a reprimand from the engineer due to personnel issues. The coppersmith – Mr Henderson – had been inattentive in his work and Stevenson blamed Selkirk for not keeping him on task: 'Instead of the work being advanced it is now behind… no working man comes to that work but I hold you responsible for his conduct.'

The lightroom floor arrived in Fraserburgh in the second week of September, delivered as always by the tender *Pharos*. The lantern was quickly assembled on the tower with the glazier being called upon by the last week of that month. Stevenson, by this stage, was keen to have the works completed: 'From the temporary nature of the present light at this season of the year – I am desirous how soon the Reflecting Apparatus can be got in place.' This reflecting apparatus was another improvement at Kinnaird as Thomas Smith's outdated reflectors were replaced with Stevenson's own new design. Instead of plaster moulds and tinned glass, Stevenson's reflectors were composed of a parabolic copper bowl with an inner layer of highly polished silver. Each reflector had a diameter of two feet and burned with an argand lamp using cylindrical wicks which gave a more brilliant light.

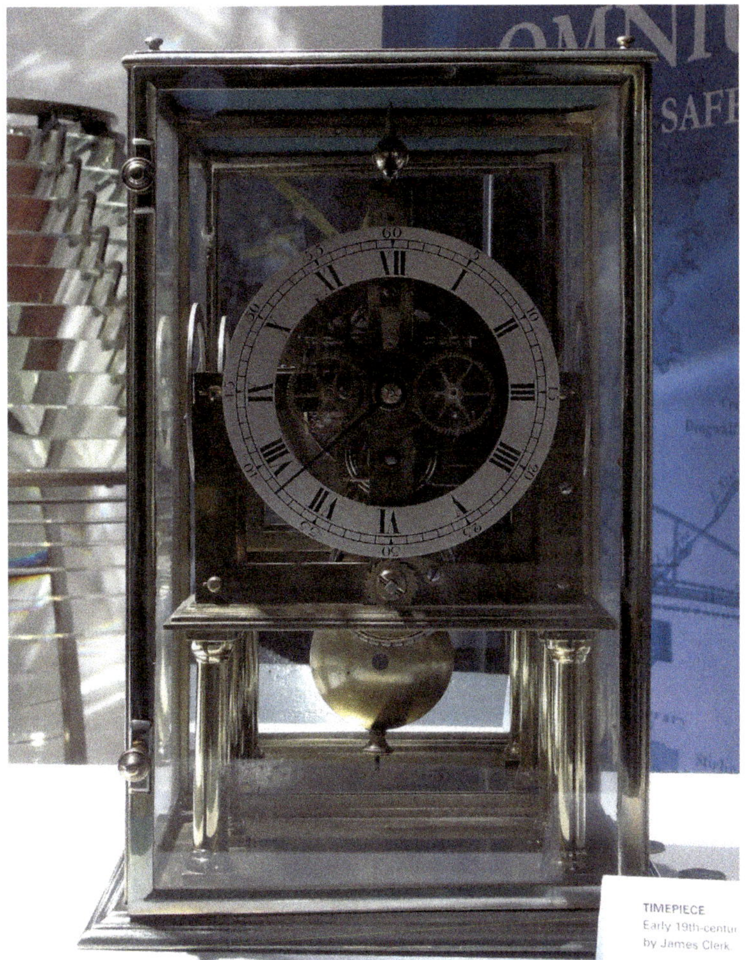

Following the improvements in 1823 the lightroom was graced with a timepiece similar to this that kept the date as well as the time. (Northern Lighthouse Board)

TIMEPIECE
Early 19th-centur
by James Clerk

Initially the reflectors used at Kinnaird were 'inferior' second-hand ones – spare reflectors gathered from other lights around the country. They were used 'until the respective operations were entirely finished, as the dust which unavoidably flies around would have spoiled the lustre of the new ones.' Stevenson had decided, however, that Kinnaird Head would retain its former character – that being a standing light – even though flashing lights were becoming more prominent. It was not necessary due to Kinnaird's seclusion from other lights on the north-east corner. The reflectors must have been installed through October, with Stevenson writing on 29 October: 'I am happy to find Kinnaird Head is now lighted.'

Professional Service

While Kinnaird Head had a new lighthouse, her Principal Lightkeeper was now an old man. Stevenson reported to the Board in January 1824 that Gray 'being now in his 74th year is unable to perform any part of the duty of cleaning and trimming the new Reflectors and Lamps owing to the somewhat paralysed state of his hands and general weakness.' He further implored the commissioners to place Gray on the list of superannuants, mentioning his twenty-five years of service, seventeen of which were as sole keeper. He finished with an impassioned plea:

The reporter begs only further to be permitted to state that few situations are more helpless than that of a discharged lightkeeper who had been for a long period in some manner abstracted from a knowledge of the world, and as the Lighthouses are all furnished by the Board, he has everything to provide on leaving his charge, as it were the world begins anew.

On 4 February 1824 Stevenson wrote to Gray informing him of his retirement but, perhaps saving the old keeper's dignity, told him it was due to the new apparatus: 'You are no doubt aware that it will be necessary to appoint a keeper more familiar with its management.' Gray was given a yearly annuity of 42 guineas and lived the remainder of his life in Fraserburgh. His replacement, Mr Peter Ewing, became the first Principal

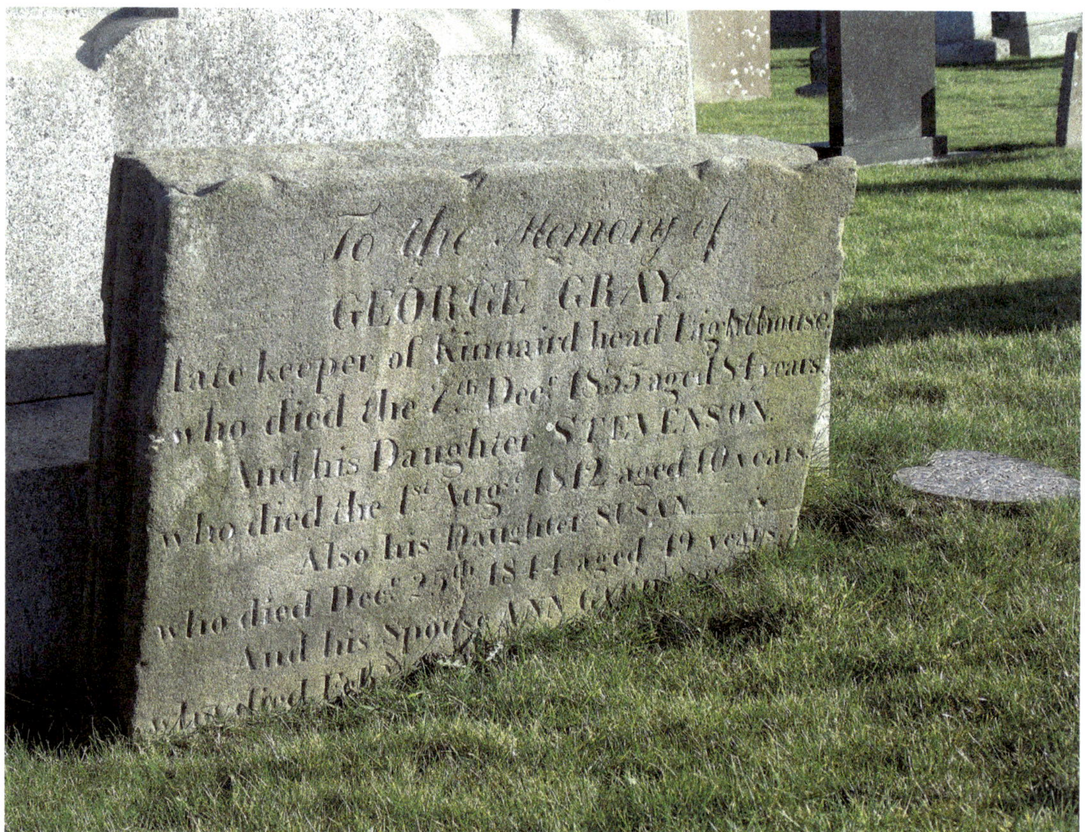

George Gray died in Fraserburgh in December 1835 – eleven years after retirement. His grave shows that he and his wife had a daughter in 1802 who they named 'Stevenson' in honour of Robert. This suggests the men thought highly of one another, which may explain why Robert fought for a generous pension for the old keeper.

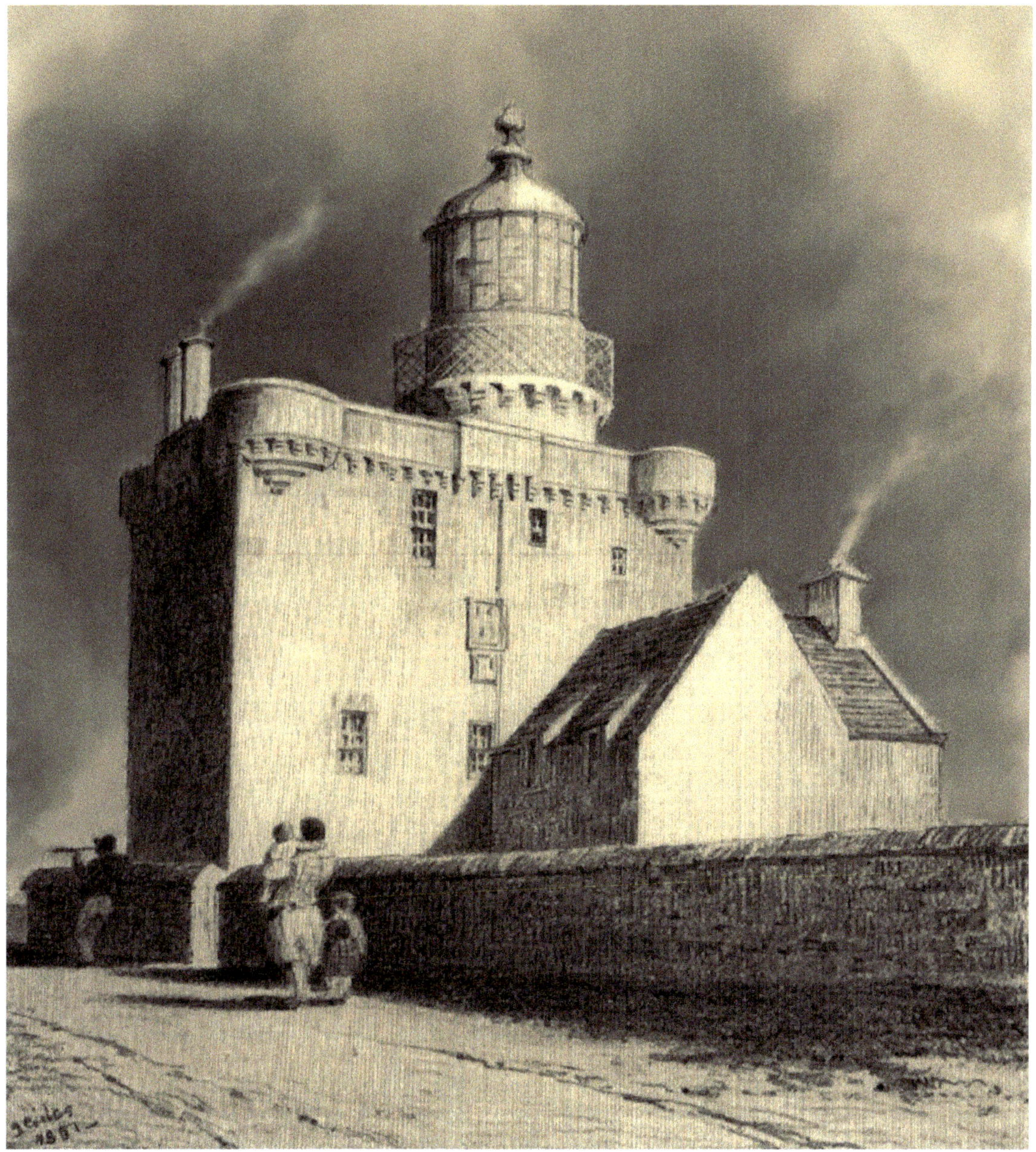

An image showing the lighthouse following Robert Stevenson's improvements. The lantern has square lantern panes while the smoke from the chimney shows the keepers were still inhabiting the old castle buildings. (James Giles, 1851)

Lightkeeper at Fraserburgh to have previous lighthouse experience. He had served as Storekeeper at Granton before being appointed an Assistant Keeper at the Bell Rock in about 1817, where he will have become acquainted with the new-style reflectors. This marked the beginning of the professional, time-served keepers who would now regularly come and go from the newly improved light at Kinnaird Head.

Chapter 4

Bright Lights

Robert Stevenson retired as Engineer to the Northern Lighthouse Board in 1843. The mantle of Engineer would pass to his eldest son Alan who, mirroring his father's elevation in 1808, was in the finishing stages of his own masterpiece at the time of his appointment. Skerryvore lighthouse, still Scotland's tallest, was built on the wild west coast some twelve miles off the island of Tiree. Often described as the world's most beautiful or perfect lighthouse, its unforgiving location had prompted Sir Walter Scott to comment some years earlier that even the Bell Rock would be a joke compared to any light built on the reef at Skerryvore!

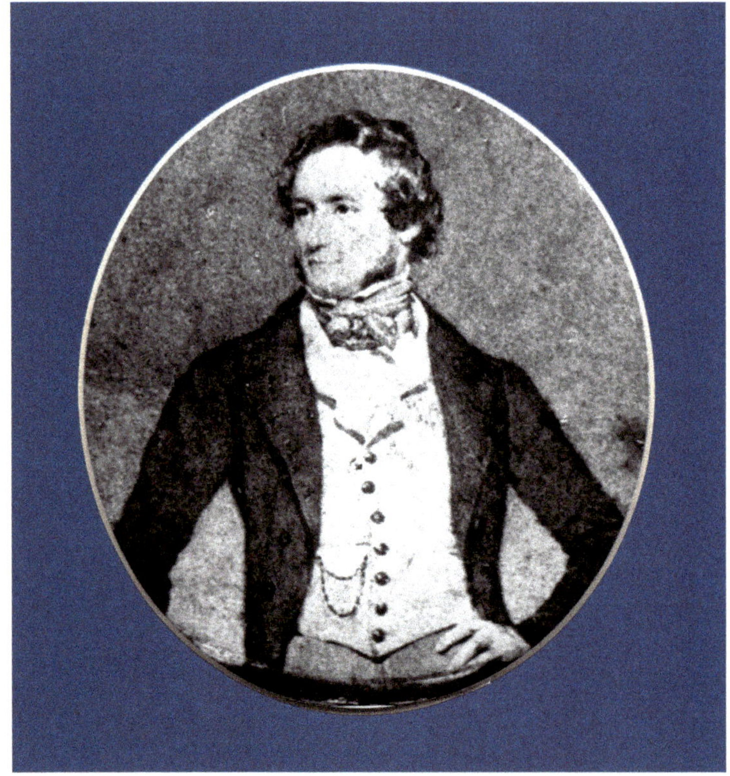

Alan Stevenson (1807–1865) succeeded his father as Engineer to the Northern Lighthouse Board in 1843. (Reproduced by kind permission of the late Quentin Stevenson)

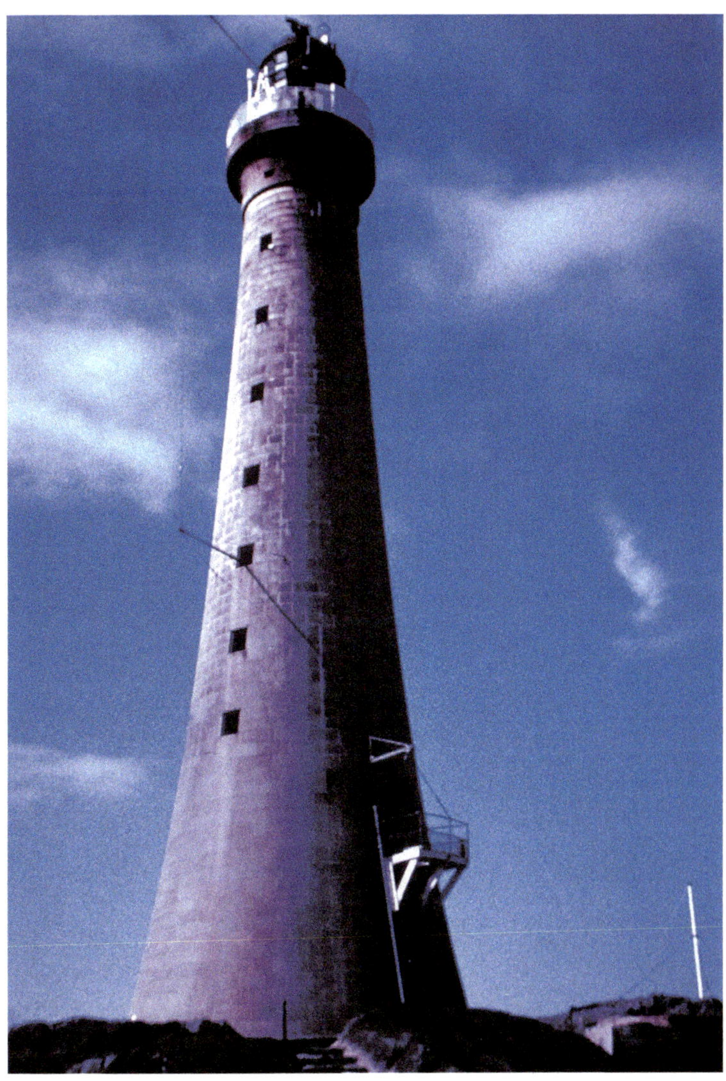

The lighthouse at Skerryvore was Alan's masterpiece. Described as the most perfect lighthouse in the world, it is still Scotland's tallest at 156 feet.

During his ten years as engineer Alan would build an astounding thirteen major lighthouses. Alan's duties included more than building alone. Like his father before him, as Engineer, he was entrusted to undertake inspection tours of all Scotland's lights to ensure the keepers were maintaining the high standards expected, but also to investigate which stations were most in need of repair or upgrade. As early as 1844 Alan reported that he found Kinnaird Head to be 'in not very good order' and 'arranged for repairs to the buildings and machinery'. The accommodation at Kinnaird Head, still being apartments of the old castle, was sub-standard for the service, but the new Engineer's main focus was on improving and upgrading the lighting apparatus.

As well as being a gifted engineer, from the mid-1830s Alan had experimented with and advocated the use of Fresnel lenses as the most brilliant means of lighthouse illumination. Kinnaird Head, still one of the major lights of the east, continued to be illuminated using parabolic reflectors. In January 1851 Alan reported to the commissioners that 'every season brings fresh proof of the necessity of the renewal of the apparatus at Kinnaird Head, which is one of the least efficient on the coast.' He required the sum of £1,158 to undertake the work, assuring the commissioners that 'such a sum is fully justified by the great importance of the headland which this lighthouse illuminates.' His request for funds was approved by the Board in May 1851 and a month later a notice to mariners was issued to advise of the works to be undertaken: 'The Commissioners of Northern Lighthouses resolved to substitute Dioptric Apparatus for the Reflectors now in use at Kinnairdhead Lighthouse.'

Alan was to install a first order dioptric apparatus – that being the largest size of lens available at that time – imported from one of the major French lens manufacturers. The dioptric lens was shaped like a cylindrical bee-hive – a cage of glass which towered about nine feet in height. The size of a first order required the light-source to be 920 mm from the glass lens, meaning the full diameter of the lens was 184 cm. It was composed of a solid belt of glass around the centre, with upper and lower prisms catching and bending the light in parallel to the central belt. While this lens was impressive, it was

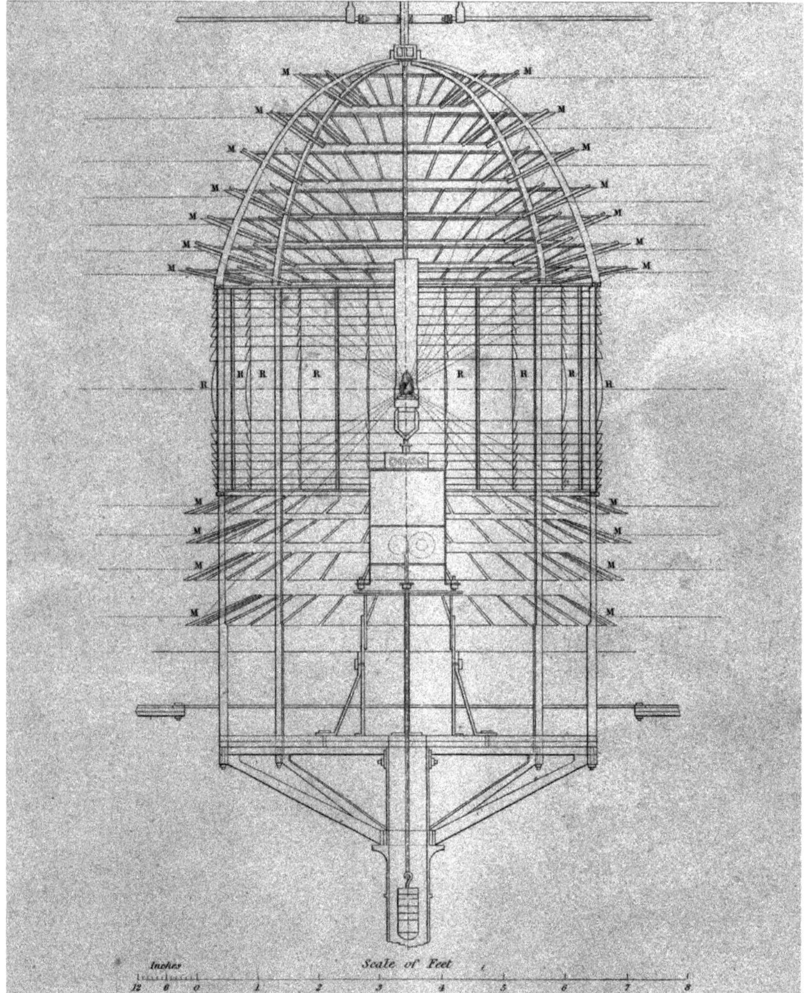

Diagram of a
1st Order dioptric
lens, as installed
at Kinnaird Head
Lighthouse in
1851, which
produced a fixed
white light.
(Alan Stevenson's
Account of
Skerryvore
Lighthouse)

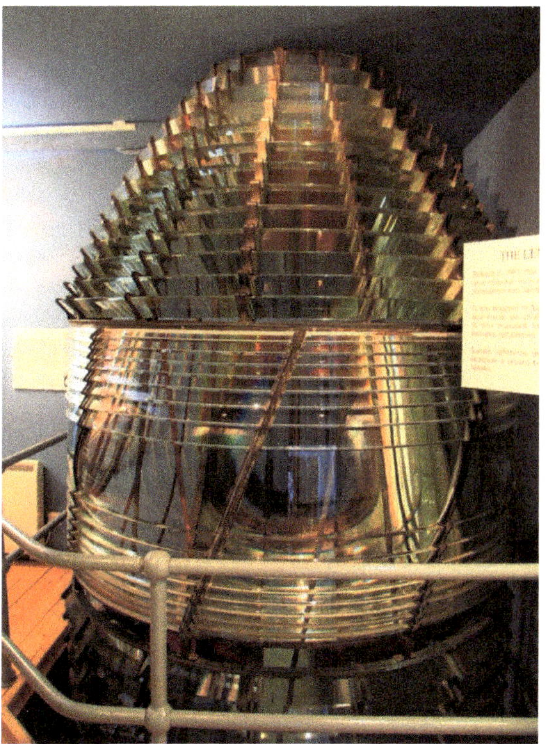

The original Kinnaird Head lens is now
lost, however it was almost exactly
the same in size and design to the lens
installed at Ardnamurchan in 1849.
(Collection of the Museum of Scottish
Lighthouses, Fraserburgh)

by no means the most advanced for the time. The lens would give only a fixed light as
before: it was stationery, and therefore would not flash. Indeed, Alan had installed the
pinnacle of lens technology at his lights at Skerryvore and Covesea Skerries in 1844 and
1847 respectively: rotating bullseye panels with his lower prisms. It may be that lack of
funds meant Kinnaird Head would wait another fifty years for a flashing apparatus to
be introduced.

Installing a first order lens also had implications to the external look of the lighthouse.
Not only was the 1823 lantern now too small for such a large apparatus, but also
outdated. When built by Robert only twenty-five years earlier, the lantern panes were
square as was conventional for the time. In 1849 Alan had adopted diagonal astragals
for the lantern resulting in triangular lantern panes. He realised that triangular astragals
were architecturally more sound and stronger than their square predecessors meaning the
gunmetal they were made from could be narrower. As such there would be less shadow to
the light as it beamed out from the lantern. The vast majority of the Northern Lighthouse
Board's towers are now crowned with lanterns of triangular panes for that reason.

When the Engineer passed for his summer visit on 15 July 1851, he found that the
whole of the old lantern was removed with only the frame of the new lantern being
erected. Despite this lack of a closed lantern, a temporary light was still being exhibited
by means of a solar wick. The works were finally completed in the middle of September
1851. Alan's diary entry that day makes it clear that, much like his father in 1823, he
was not impressed with the time it had taken: 'John Robertson has been here with 4 men
for more than 3 months. I must truly try to make some change for I will not have this
kind of delay and dozing again. I am sure they have misused their time.'

While the contractors came in for his scorn, he gave the new dioptric apparatus a mixed review with his personal diary on 23 September 1851 recording:

> We see Kinnairdhead about 10 miles off as we turn the point of Rosehearty and although it is a fine light I think it inferior to Pentland Skerries in a very considerable degree. We land about 9.45 and find Mr Cornochan on watch. The flame is good and in examining the prisms I find them to fill very well even to the top and bottom although ofcourse much inferior to the central portion.

That was his personal reflection. On his return to Edinburgh he later reported to the commissioners, who had approved the funds for the upgrade at his request, that 'on the night of 23 September, which was rather foggy, I witnessed with satisfaction a severe trial of its power in so unfavourable a medium.'

The Keepers

During these changes Kinnaird Head was under the watch of Principal Keeper John Reid, who arrived at the station in February 1842 following the retirement of Peter Ewing. He remained at the station for seventeen years. Aptly his career had begun at Kinnaird Head where he underwent two years of training between 1817 and 1818 under the watch of George Gray. While Mr Reid came from Peterhead he has no known connection with his more famous namesake, the first Principal Lightkeeper of the Bell Rock. His duties were, though, wide ranging. As well as the serving Principal at Kinnaird Head, he described himself in 1858 as contractor of repairs for Sumburgh Head, and 'inspector at Buchanness, Cape Wrath, Dunnet Head, and Barrahead lighthouses'. Thus his duties must surely have frequently taken him away from his charge in Fraserburgh.

It may have been these absences which led the station to become run down as Alan had cause to punish keepers on two separate occasions. First, in January 1846, each lightkeeper was fined the sum of 30 shillings after the Engineer reported that the 'visit to Kinnairdhead was far from being satisfactory, as I found the lightroom in a state which satisfied me that there had been considerable intermission of that attention to the details of the Lightroom duty.' It seems the keepers had not been undertaking the expected standard of cleanliness at the station. Again, in January 1850, the Engineer reported that 'during the indisposition of the Principal Lightkeeper at Kinnairdhead, when the whole responsibility of the management of the Establishment devolved upon the Assistant Lightkeeper, the glass and chimneys had on one occasion been found in a state of censure.' At the Engineer's suggestion, the commissioners fined William Lyall – assistant keeper – one guinea, before shifting him off to Loch Ryan – a minor station by comparison – later that year.

Kinnaird Head was still a two-man system, and as such in Mr Reid's absence the occasional keeper would be called to the lighthouse to cover. Regulation stated the Board would provide 'at least one person resident near the lighthouse, who shall come under an agreement to be always ready to take the place of either keeper in case of sickness or other emergency.' These men would have other employment, with the lighthouse work being a secondary income. For a period in the mid-1840s one of the occasionals was Lewis Proctor, a harbour labourer with a young family to keep. Unfortunately, to add to Kinnaird's poor reputation, in 1847 he 'met with a severe accident by a fall from the lighthouse at

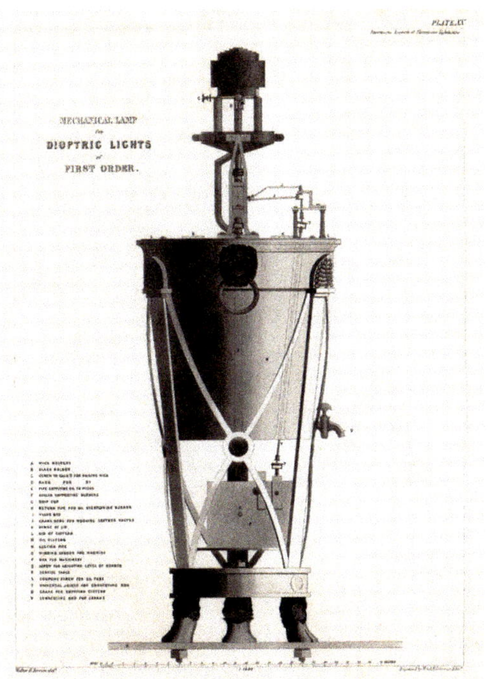

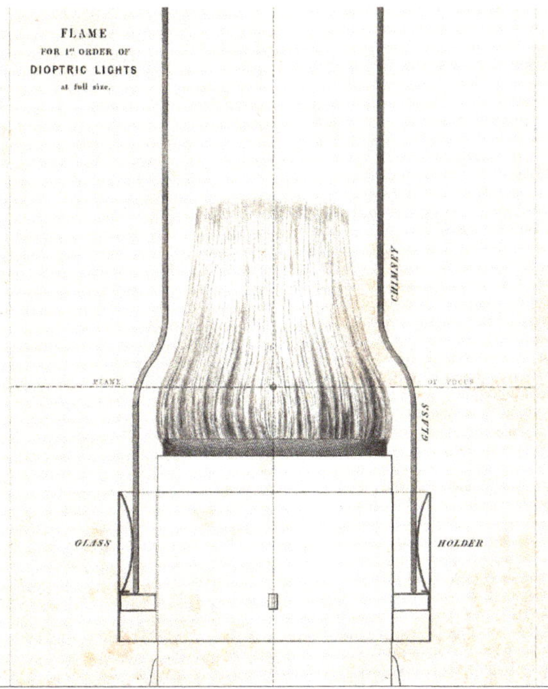

Above left: Some of Alan Stevenson's colza mechanical lamps had classical flourishes, however it is likely that Kinnaird's oil cistern was much plainer. The lamp had to be wound at regular intervals to ensure a constant supply of colza oil to the burner. (Alan Stevenson's Account of Skerryvore Lighthouse)

Above right: Every lightroom that used the new mechanical lamps was provided with an illustration of how high the flame should sit in the glass chimney. Pictured is the flame height for the 1st Order apparatus. (Alan Stevenson's Account of Skerryvore Lighthouse)

Kinnairdshead.' While the details of the accident are not recorded, the most common cause of a severe fall occurred when cleaning exterior lantern panes. The Board's accounts of 1848 show he was given a gratuity of £30 as compensation for his inability to work. The Fraserburgh poor records suggest he died in August 1850 aged thirty-two, leaving his four children – the eldest of whom was under ten – as orphans on the poor register.

Accommodation

The full-time keepers at Kinnaird Head were handsomely paid. In the 1840s a Principal Keeper drew a salary of £47, while his assistant received £37. The keepers at Kinnaird Head, though, had much to be disgruntled about as part of the package was normally a purpose-built, furnished house. For one reason or another this had not come to full fruition at Kinnaird as the keepers were still living in the castle buildings, which had been noted as poor some sixty years earlier. The 1841 census shows that two keepers' families were crammed into the old castle accommodation; fourteen people in total. The seventy-year-old Principal Peter Ewing, his wife, son, daughter, son-in-law, and two grandchildren in one part, with assistant James Lindsay and his wife and five children in the other. By 1851 there were only eight inhabitants as Mr Reid's assistant at the time had no family, but by then the Engineer had taken note of this unhappy situation.

After viewing the upgrade works of 1851 Alan noted in his diary that 'new houses are truly much wanted here'. Before his medical retirement in 1853, Alan saw the initial planning of having new accommodation built for the keepers with a notice for contractors being issued on 4 January 1853. The building of the houses would be overseen by his brothers and successors, David and Thomas Stevenson, who would serve as joint engineers to the Board. The new houses would be of the standard design seen around the coast of Scotland. Specifically designed for harsh coastal conditions with thick walls and heavy lead roofs, the keepers must have felt an immense difference from the draughty and leaky castle buildings. The cottages, semi-detached, each had two bedrooms and a kitchen, as well as one other good room. While this may not seem spacious for a large family (John Reid had a wife and four children in 1851) it was luxury compared to general standards in Scotland at that time: in 1861 about 64 per cent of the Scottish population was living in one- or two-roomed accommodation. The Kinnaird Head houses were provided rent free, with allowances given to provide free coal and oil for heat and lighting of these new buildings.

If the engineers believed improved conditions were going to enhance standards and discipline at Kinnaird Head they were sadly mistaken. As the 1850s progressed,

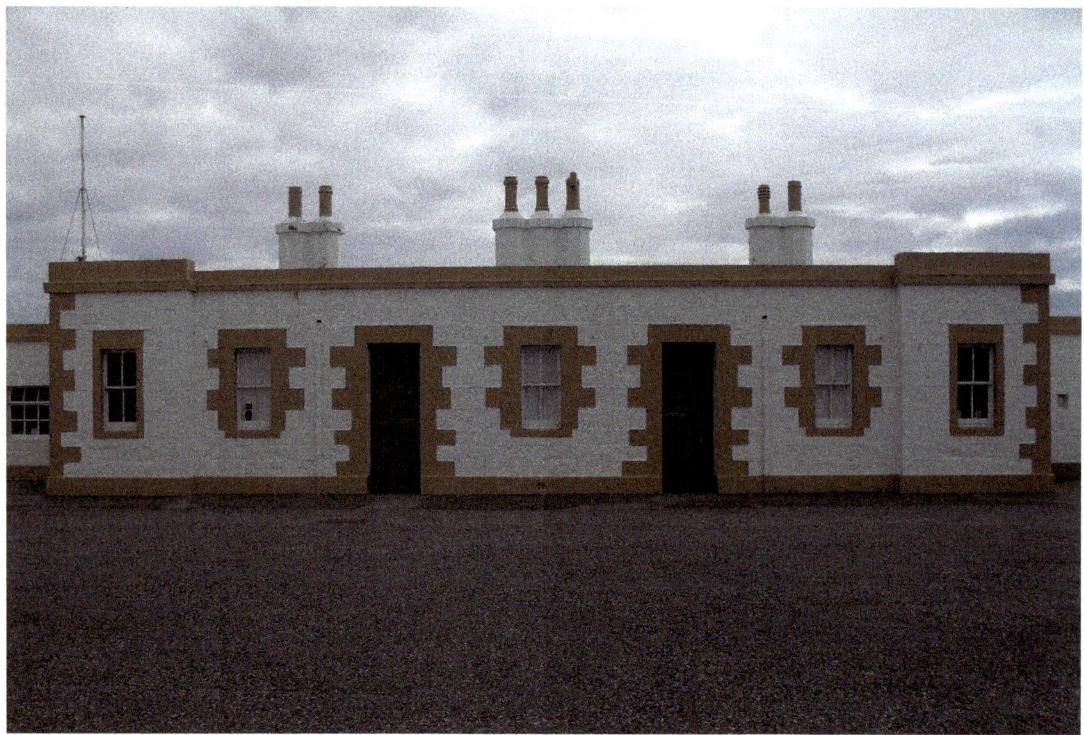

In 1853 the lightkeepers at Kinnaird Head finally moved out of the old castle apartments into comfortable, purpose-built, NLB standard cottages.

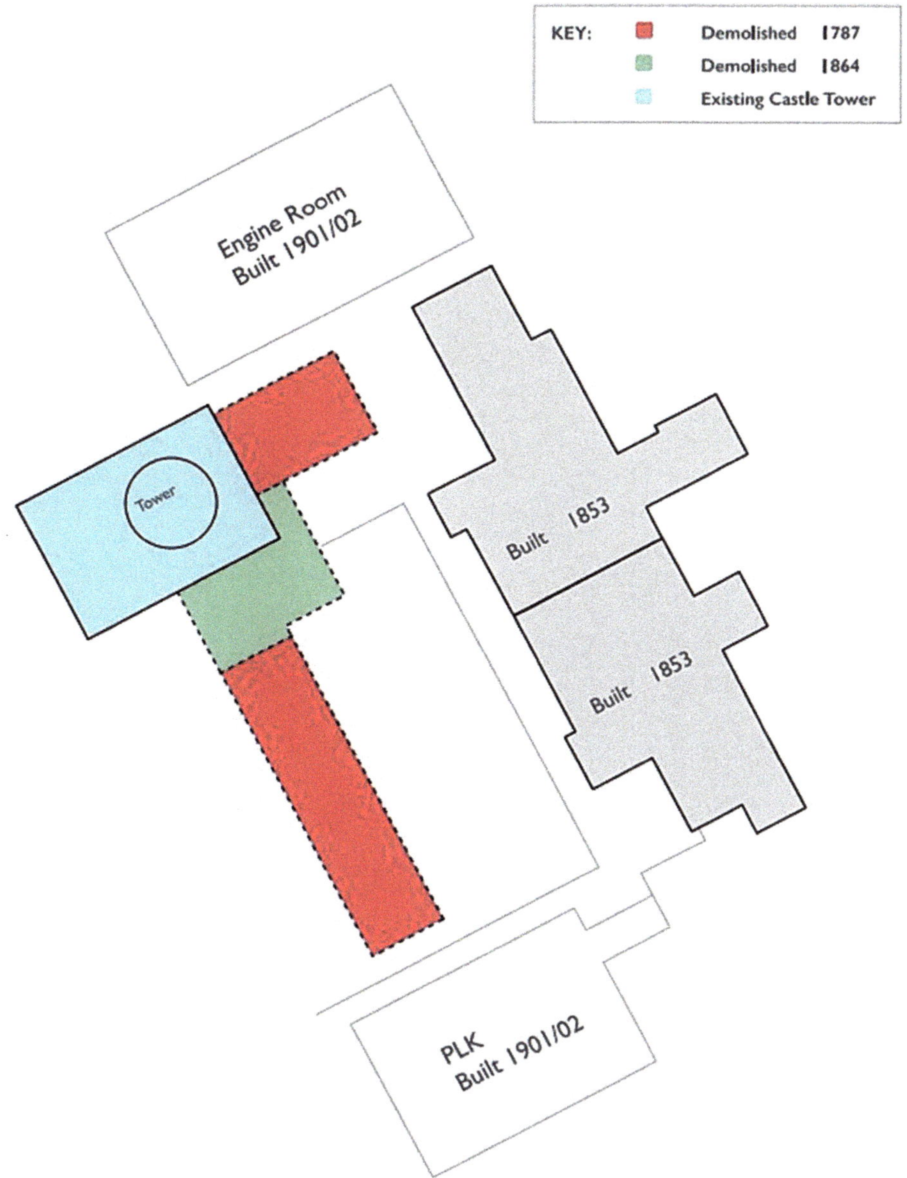

While the cottages were built in 1853, the old castle 'low buildings' were not demolished until 1864. This plan shows the demolition of the castle and later additions to the site. (With thanks to Calum MacLeod)

either due to the lax attitude of the Principal Mr Reid, or indeed due to his absence, two assistants found themselves falling foul of regulations. In October 1856 the commissioners received a report that the light at Kinnaird Head had been 'endangered and its efficiency very much impaired'. The Assistant Keeper on watch, William Shearer, had blamed defects in the new mechanical lamp for the poor light causing the commissioners to investigate. The first point in the Lightkeeper's instructions was fairly clear: 'Lightkeepers shall receive a regular written appointment, but they are to understand that they are engaged from day to day at the pleasure of the commissioners, and on cause shown may be instantly dismissed.' For endangering the light Mr Shearer could expect the commissioners to 'award such punishment as to them shall see fit.' Unfortunately for Mr Shearer, the commissioners found no issue with the lamp, and instead decided 'that either from being asleep on his post, or from some other gross negligence, the Lightkeeper on Watch allowed the weight to run down, and the machine to come to a stand.' For this offence, William Shearer was dismissed.

Months after Mr Reid's retirement in 1859, his last assistant also found himself in trouble. As was required by regulation the new Principal James Black reported Assistant Keeper Dugald McLaren for falling asleep on duty. While asleep he clearly could not wind the mechanical lamp, impeding the flow of oil, causing the light to become extinguished. Despite admitting the offence (indeed he reported himself with the Principal), regulations were clear: he had to be dismissed from the service as a warning to all other keepers of the consequences. Not only were Mr Shearer and Mr McLaren now jobless, but also required to leave their furnished, rent-free accommodation with the knowledge that no reference would be supplied from their now former employers.

As life at Kinnaird Head proved, the engineers and commissioners did their best to provide their lighthouses with the most up to date technologies available, while also maintaining their keepers in relative comfort and status. For this they expected hard work and discipline but if this was not forthcoming, failure was rarely tolerated.

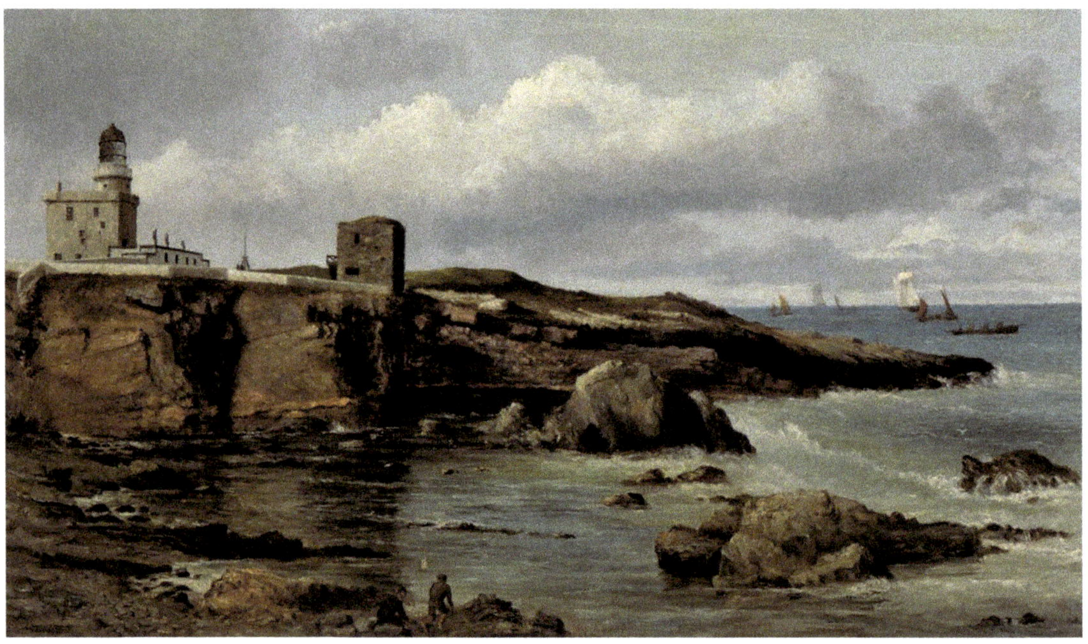

Kinnaird Head Lighthouse by 1875, showing Alan Stevenson's lantern and the new cottages. (Aberdeenshire Council Library Service)

Chapter 5

The Paraffin Oilers

Despite the vast improvement at the lighthouse, the north-east coast between Kinnaird Head and Buchan Ness, near Peterhead, remained treacherous due to its rocky nature – particularly at Cairnbulg and Rattray Head. As early as 1848 Alan Stevenson wrote that 'an important benefit would be conferred on Navigation' if a beacon were built on the Cairnbulg Briggs as 'various persons have expressed a desire for a small light somewhere on the line of coast between Buchanness and Kinnairdhead.' Due to the vast expansion of the service in other areas around Scotland that part of the coast would remain in

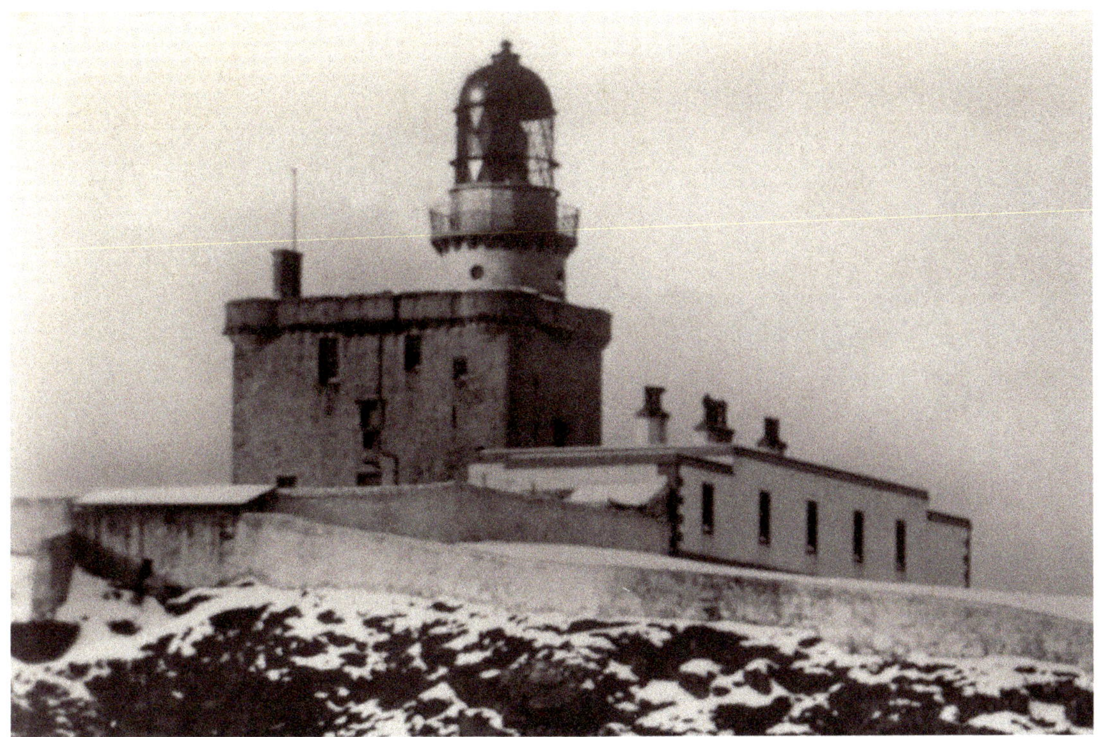

A rare photograph of Kinnaird Head *c.* 1900. Between 1853 and 1902 very little additional building work was carried out at the station.

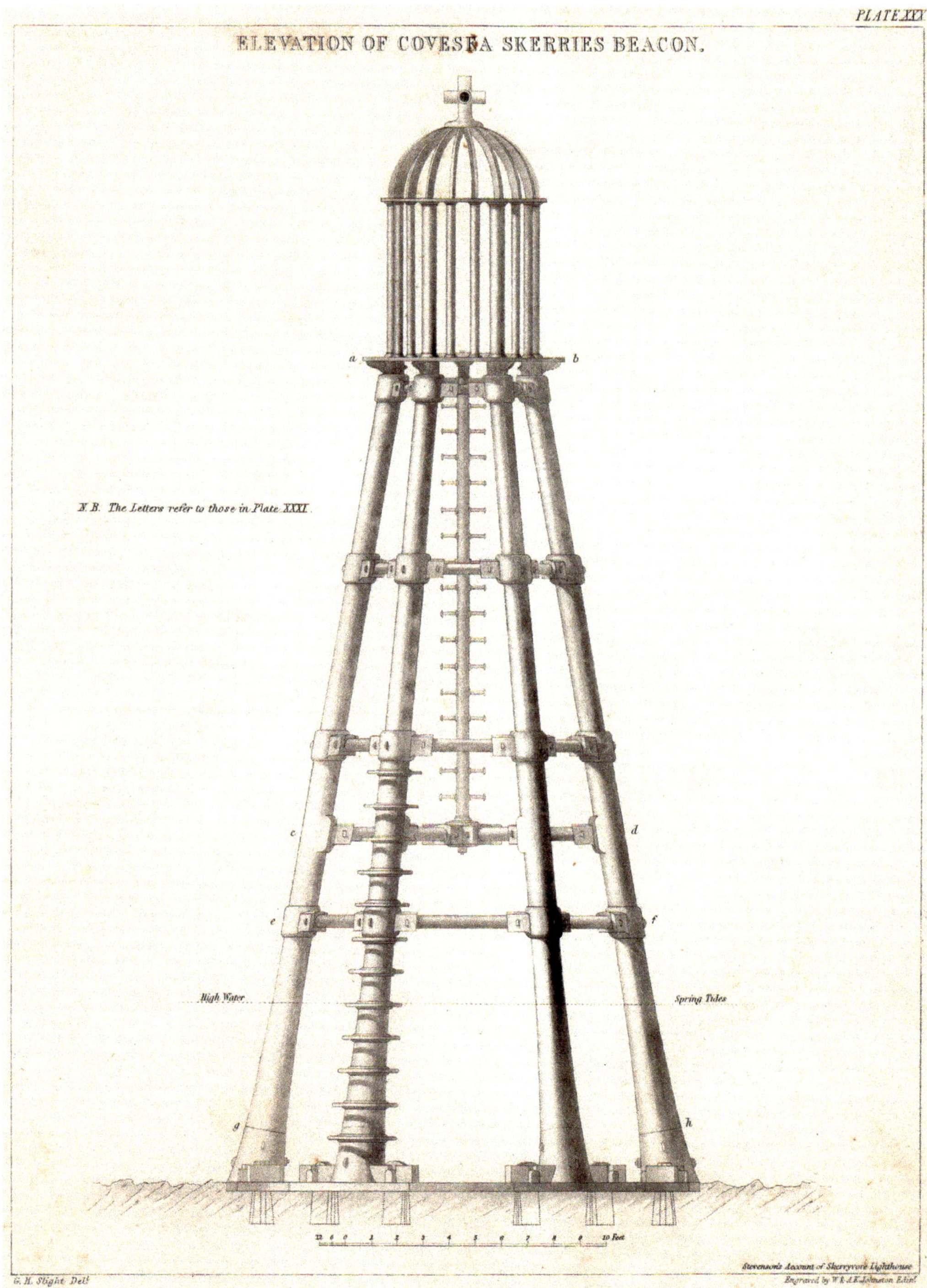

Plan of the cage beacon built off Covesea Skerries, Lossiemouth. A beacon of a similar design was erected on the Cairnbulg Briggs, at the opposite end of the bay of Fraserburgh, in 1858. (Alan Stevenson's Account of Skerryvore Lighthouse)

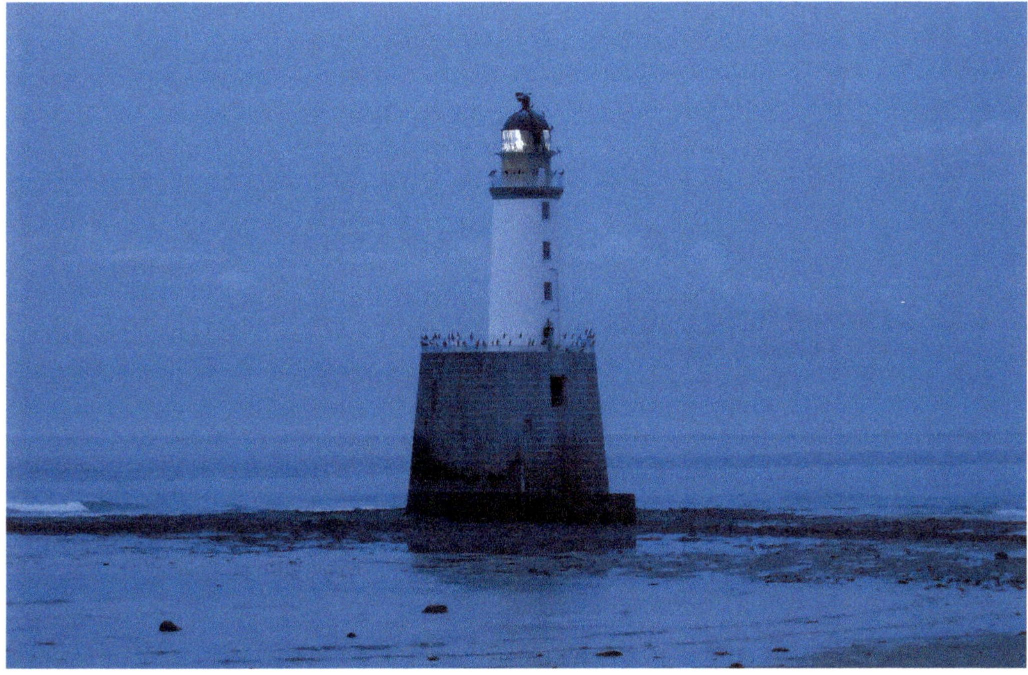

The Rattray Briggs was not marked with a lighthouse until 1895 (pictured) but a red sector was created on Kinnaird Head's lantern to warn ships of the dangers of Rattray when approaching from the south.

the darkness for the next fifty years. At Cairnbulg in 1858 the commissioners built a cheaper unlit cage beacon, the purpose of the structure being that if a vessel did founder on the rocks the crew could cling to the iron cage while awaiting rescue. Fraserburgh had, from 1858, the RNLI's first official operational lifeboat station in Scotland. Regarding Rattray Head the Fraserburgh Coastguard, Commander Beatson, made the suggestion that Kinnaird should exhibit a red sector to vessels sailing north up the coast. The commissioners were agreeable and so from 1 January 1862 Kinnaird Head's character of fixed white was slightly altered. The notice read that 'the light on Kinnaird Head will be changed to red colour, from the bearing of about N. W. by N. ½ N., as far to the Westward as the land will permit it to be seen; but in every other direction it will continue to be of the natural colour as at present.'

Lighthouse Life

These cheaper alternatives to new lights were likely preferred by the commissioners due to the expense incurred by the great expansion of the service over that period. In 1852 the light was already one of thirty-four managed by the Northern Lighthouse Board; by 1875 it was only one of sixty-two. Expansion was expensive; more lights would mean more keepers were employed by the NLB. The effect on Kinnaird Head would be that following John Reid most keepers were based at the station for an average of

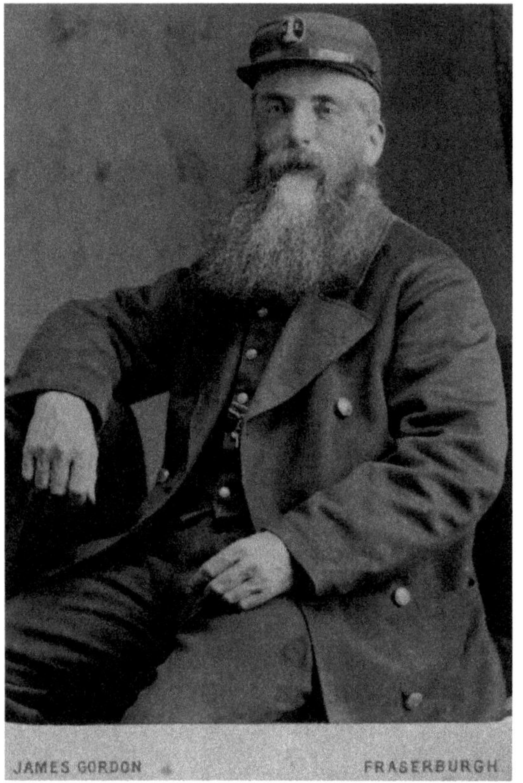

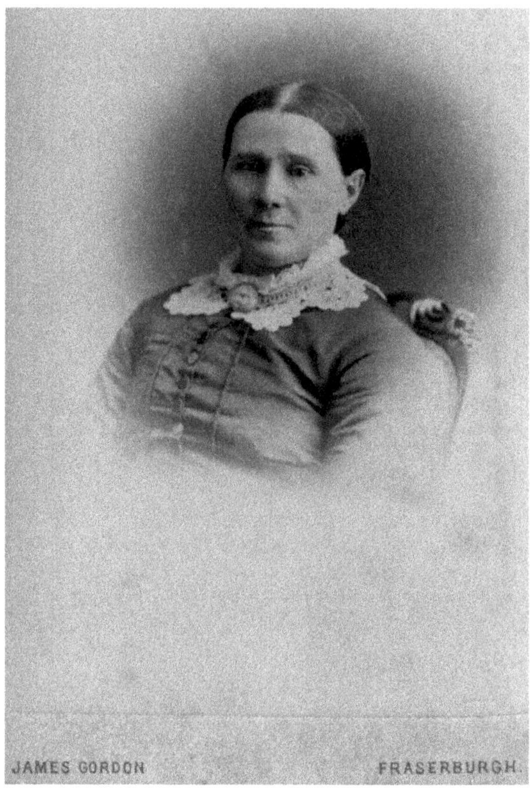

Above left: David M. Scott served as assistant at Kinnaird Head 1870–1883. As a career keeper he served at seven different stations over thirty-two years, including lighthouses at Lewis, Shetland, Aberdeenshire and Arran. (Courtesy of Mr Gordon Milne)

Above right: When the keeper was shifted, the family had to follow. With seven children to care for, Mrs Jessie Scott most likely considered herself lucky to be based at Kinnaird Head for thirteen years. She married Mr Scott in 1859, when he had settled employment as a sailmaker at Arbroath. *(Courtesy of Mr Gordon Milne)*

only four years or less before being transferred. Between 1859 and 1869 three Principal Lightkeepers and five assistants had served Kinnaird Head before being sent to new lights around every part of the coast of Scotland. There was a brief period of stability with the arrival of Principal Keeper Francis Harvey in 1869, and assistant David M. Scott in 1870. Both would serve Kinnaird Head for over a decade (seventeen years in the case of Harvey), with both living the lives of typical career keepers.

The 1871 census for Kinnaird Head shows that eighteen people were living in the two fully furnished, rent-free semi-detached keepers' cottages. That fact alone, given that the houses only had two bedrooms, was astounding – but more interesting were the recorded entries for place of birth. For the eighteen people – consisting of two families – there were eight different places of birth: Campbelltown; Leith; Fraserburgh; Orkney; Caithness; Arbroath; Ross-shire; and Stornoway. This was, of course, caused by the keepers continually receiving orders to move on to new stations. Mr Scott, for example, had entered the service in 1863 with Kinnaird Head being his fourth station in seven years. As time went on this lack of a home town led to the lightkeepers and (more especially) their children being referred to as 'Paraffin Oilers'. They generally did not remain anywhere long enough to call home, and so they belonged to the lighthouse community.

This community could be quite tight-knit, as shown in the case of Mr Harvey. He was married while serving as assistant at the Pentland Skerries lighthouse. His bride was the daughter of his Principal Keeper meaning that Principal and Assistant were now father and son-in-law, his new wife simply flitting next door. Intermarriage between families would be a common thing for much of the nineteenth century, likely caused by the secluded nature of many of the lighthouse complexes. We can only wonder what Robert Stevenson would have made of such arrangements! As for Mr Scott, he was one of many second or third generations now to be in the employment of the NLB. He was born into the lighthouse service at the Signal Tower in Arbroath; his father was boatman for the Bell Rock lighthouse.

Mr Harvey, the Principal, was by all accounts a well-liked and respected member of the community. At the time of his retirement in 1887 it was noted that 'he was a very painstaking and careful official' who 'has never been "off duty" one day through ill health.' He became popular with locals due to 'the kindly and neighbourly feeling that prompted him to leave the beautiful greens that surround the castle open to the public, when, if he had wished, they could have been excluded.' Sadly, this kind act may have been caused by a personal tragedy. In May 1870 a broken iron gate had been left leaning on the lighthouse boundary dyke when his four-year-old daughter, Williamina, started to climb on the iron frame. The heavy gate overbalanced and fell on top of her, breaking her spine causing instantaneous death. The gates, it seems, were thereafter quickly removed altogether.

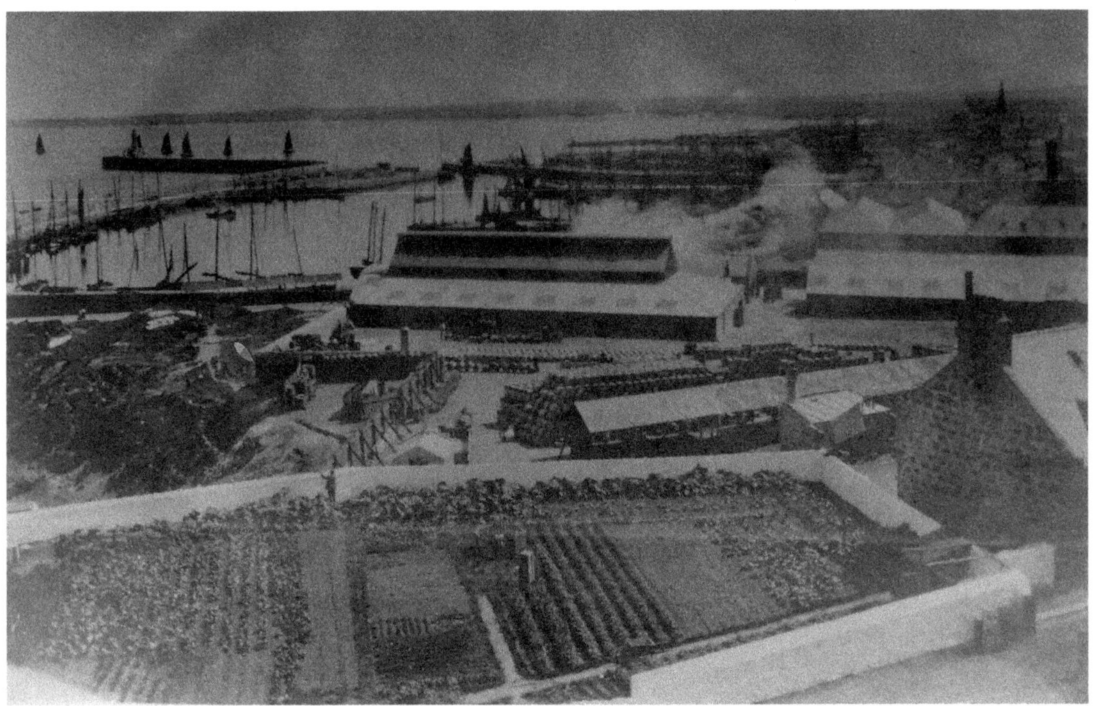

View from Kinnaird Head Lighthouse looking south *c.* 1890. The lighthouse vegetable garden, created by Mr Harvey in the 1870s, can be seen.

In addition to the castle greens at Kinnaird Head, keepers around Scotland had plots of land on which they could grow vegetables to supplement their diets, though plots at Kinnaird Head had always been judged to be too poor for growing an adequate crop. As the keepers did not have this benefit they were given an additional annual allowance of £10, which the commissioners often had to remind them was intended to provide a varied diet – the money often being spent on other non-essentials! In 1880, however, Harvey improved the gardens at Kinnaird by laying new soil at a cost of £6 13*s* 6*d*, resulting in a magnificent walled garden of fresh vegetables for the keepers' benefit. This was indeed a saving for the commissioners, as the annual allowance would now be surrendered. It is unknown if Mr Harvey's then assistant was agreeable to this new arrangement!

Supplying the Light

By the 1880s Kinnaird Head Castle was no longer a remote structure surrounded by acres of greens. Indeed by 1885 the town had grown so much to the north and east that not only were much of the old greens now occupied, but the keepers at Kinnaird Head found themselves in the still unusual situation of having non-lighthouse neighbours in the immediate vicinity of the station. The houses of Castle Terrace had reached the station's boundary walls. The lighthouse was now very much a part of the town, one well connected by road and – from 1865 – by rail. Despite this, like all other lighthouses,

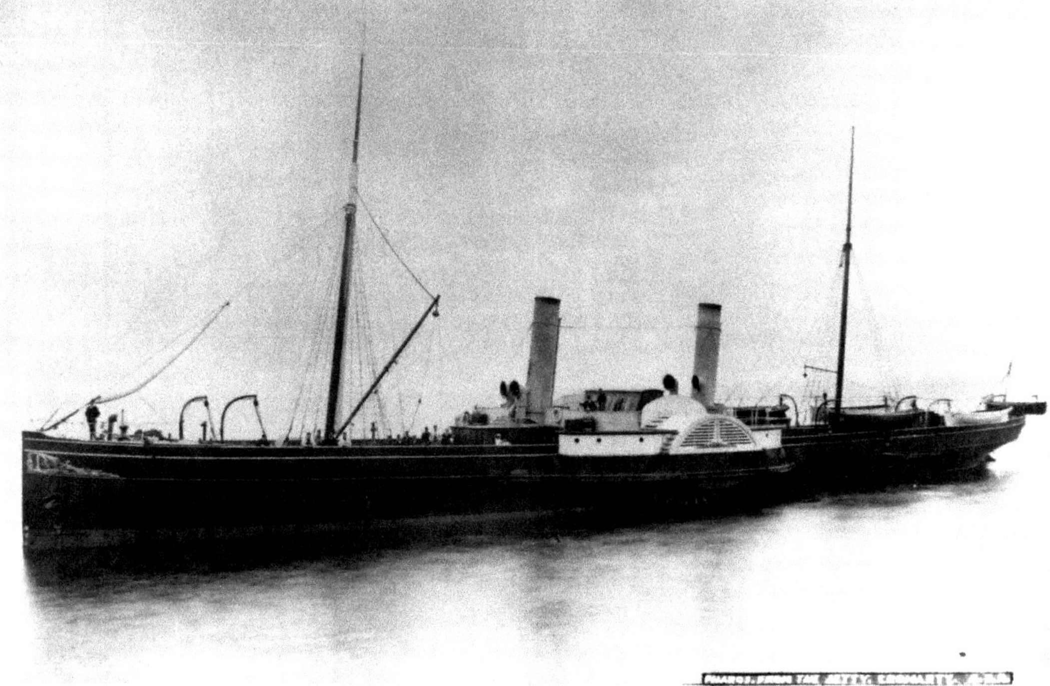

Paddle steamer *Pharos* served the NLB 1874–1909 and would have been responsible for supplying Kinnaird Head throughout that period.

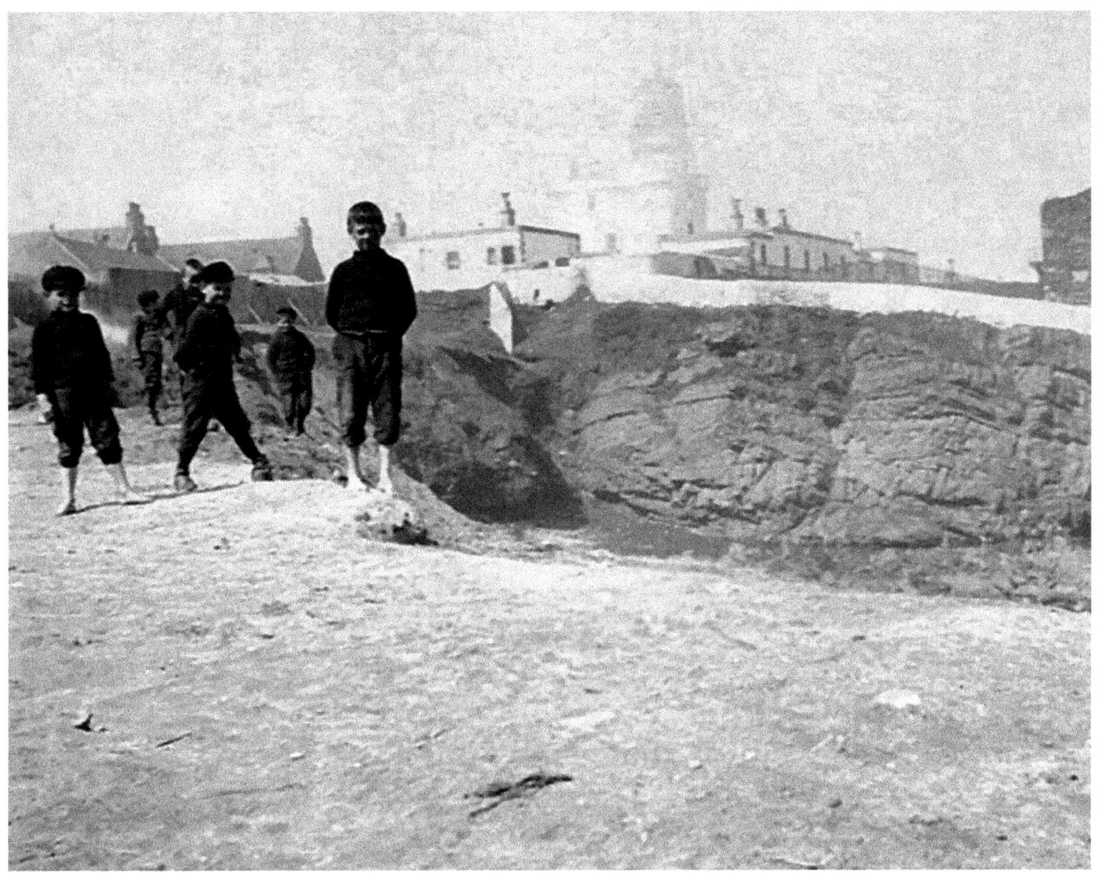

Local children look on at the commissioners as they proceed to the lighthouse from Fraserburgh Harbour following their disembarking from the Pharos *c.* 1910. (The Peddie Collection, Museum of Scottish Lighthouses/NL Heritage Trust)

the commissioners continued to supply and visit the station by using the lighthouse tenders from the sea.

From the earliest days of the service the commissioners found it easier (and apparently cheaper) to supply their lights with oil and coals by the sea. This was mainly because all supplies were obtained by tender from a central supplier by lowest bid. Between 1820 and 1846 Kinnaird Head was supplied with oil and coals by the wooden schooner *Regent*. The vessel, after delivering coals in March, was sent to London once a year to receive sixty tons of oil which she would then distribute to all Scottish lighthouses – in casks – starting with the Isle of May. With the expansion of the lighthouses from the 1840s onward, more vessels were required, each having their own particular area to service. Kinnaird, being on the east coast, was serviced mainly by the commissioners' own ship – the *Pharos* – from 1846 onward. The *Pharos* – of which there have now been ten vessels bearing that name – would normally visit Kinnaird Head two or three times a year: one visit for stores; one for oil; and if the keepers were unlucky, one for the commissioners' inspection tour.

The vessel itself never came in to Fraserburgh harbour, instead dropping anchor in Fraserburgh's bay and launching a small rowing craft to take the oil casks and other supplies to the harbour where they would be met by carters employed, again, by tender. By the turn of the twentieth century this process was almost unchanged which drew criticism from one local correspondent in the *Fraserburgh Herald*: 'Local traders would prefer the commissioners to purchase their stores in town, but official red tapism is apparently too strong to permit of such a sensible course of action.' Delivery of goods would continue in this manner until just before the Second World War.

During Harvey's tenure as Principal one key change he did oversee was the shift from burning colza oil (first used at the station in 1847) to the paraffin in 1874. From 1872, following a series of experiments with the Doty paraffin burners, David and Thomas Stevenson adopted and began installing them through all the Scottish lights. They found that the paraffin operations 'at one half the cost give an increased luminous for an equal consumption.' The NLB were the first lighthouse authority in the UK to adopt paraffin burners, giving an 'annual saving of between £4,500 and £5,000 in the maintenance of the lights on the Scotch coast.' Under the correct conditions, paraffin burned more cleanly and smoothly than the whale and colza oil operations. The paraffin was burned at Kinnaird Head for the next 100 years.

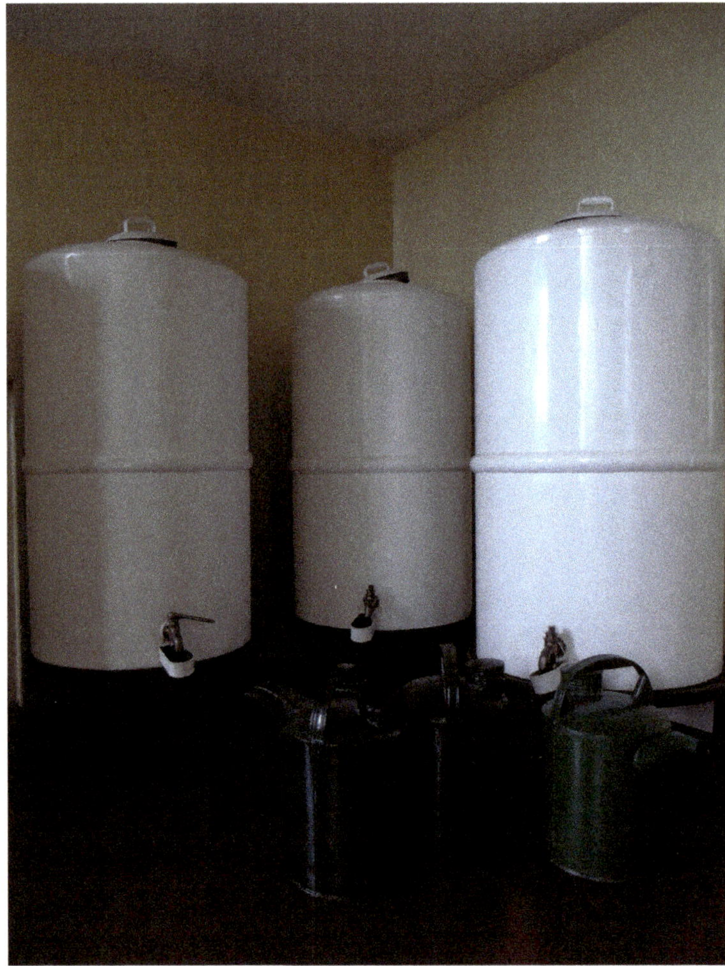

The paraffin room formerly held twelve large tanks for storing the oil. This would hold a year's supply with a month or two reserves.

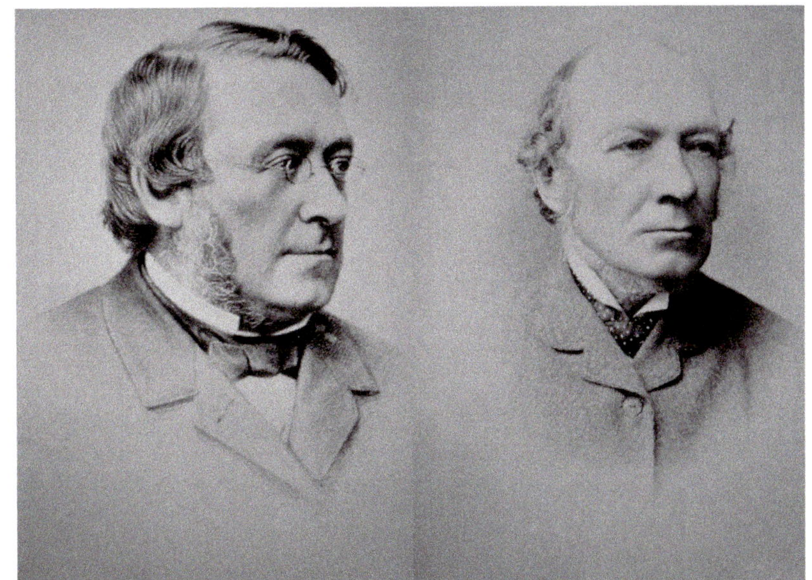

David and Thomas Stevenson introduced the paraffin lamps to the Northern Lighthouses in the 1870s. Paraffin was used in the lamps at Kinnaird Head for just over 100 years.

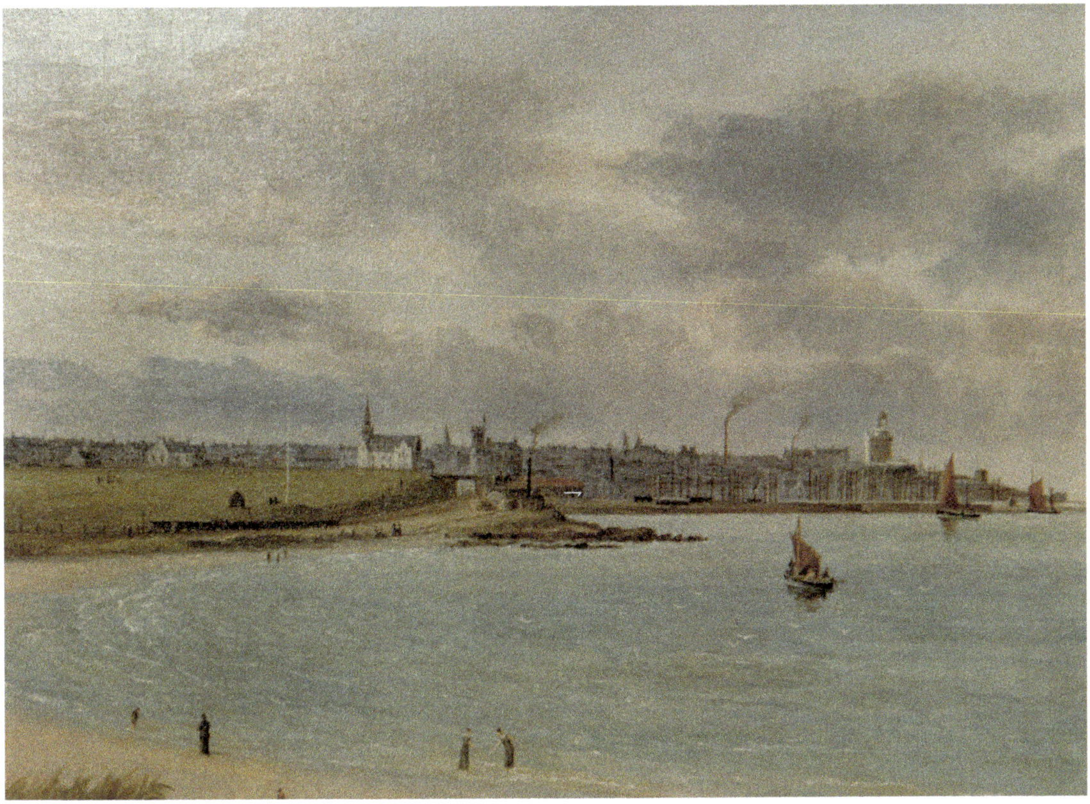

By the end of the 1880s the town of Fraserburgh had expanded to the extent that the lighthouse was no longer isolated by the old castle greens. Only the commissioners' land to the north-east of the station could be described as 'green'. (Andrew Webster, *c.* 1880)

Chapter 6

Scotland's Most Powerful Light

In 1900 David Alan Stevenson (1854–1938) paid one of his regular visits to Kinnaird Head, but this time with a view to plan major works at the station which was now well out of date. Perhaps the greatest shortcoming at Kinnaird Head was that it still exhibited the stationary light which his uncle, Alan Stevenson, had installed fifty years earlier. David, and his brother Charles Alexander (1855–1950), planned to modernise and overhaul the lightroom by introducing the pinnacle of lens technology to the station: a hyper-radial lens, the largest size of lens ever made for lighthouses.

In July 1901 the lens was ordered from the Chance Brothers' Smethwick factory, near Birmingham, at a cost of £1,270. The Chance Brothers were the only successful makers of lighthouse lenses in the British Isles, with most other lenses being made

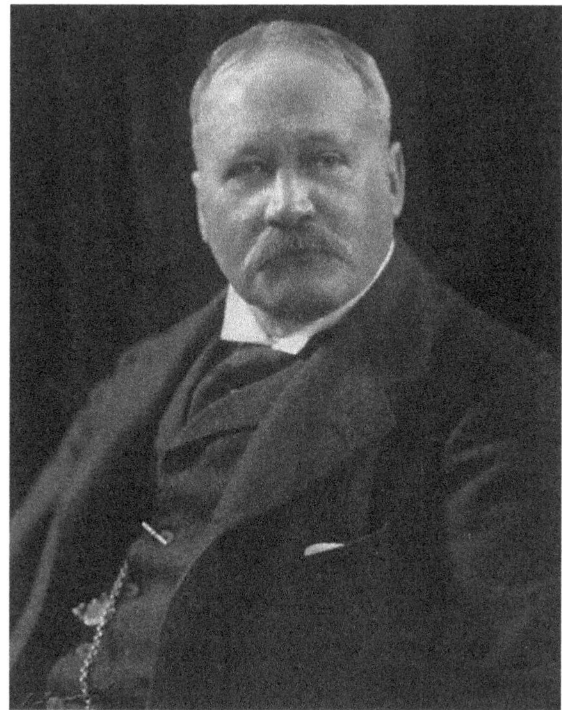

As Engineer to the Northern Lighthouse Board, David A. Stevenson oversaw the last major alterations and improvements to Kinnaird Head between 1902 and 1903.

by French companies. These hyper-radial lenses had first been proposed by Thomas Stevenson in 1869 due to the great advancement of lamps and burners. The lamps were becoming so large that first order lenses were now unable to condense the light effectively and in extreme cases the immense heat from the flame could even crack the glass. The solution was simple: make the lenses larger by extending their diameter. The size of a lens is determined by the focal distance between the light source and the lens glass, the distance between the two in a hyper-radial being 1330 mm (compared to 920 mm for a first order). In truth Kinnaird Head's is not a full hyper-radial, instead being of a rare bi-order variety. This, again, was a new specification designed by the Stevenson brothers, only being the second in operation in Scotland after that of the Bell Rock. Bi-order simply means that it was one lens composed of two different sizes. The bullseye panels were hyper-radial with the focal distance of 1330 mm, but the prisms on each side were set at first order level meaning they sat closer to the light source. Further, the bullseye panel was arranged with Charles Stevenson's equiangular prisms, a feature which allowed the light to be better condensed into a stronger beam.

The lens is a massive structure – about four tons in weight and over 10 foot high – so for it to be installed the whole light-room and lantern had to be enlarged and rebuilt around it. The new lantern was composed of three tiers of triangular gunmetal astragals, the diameter being 18 inches larger than the old lantern. The lantern was supported on

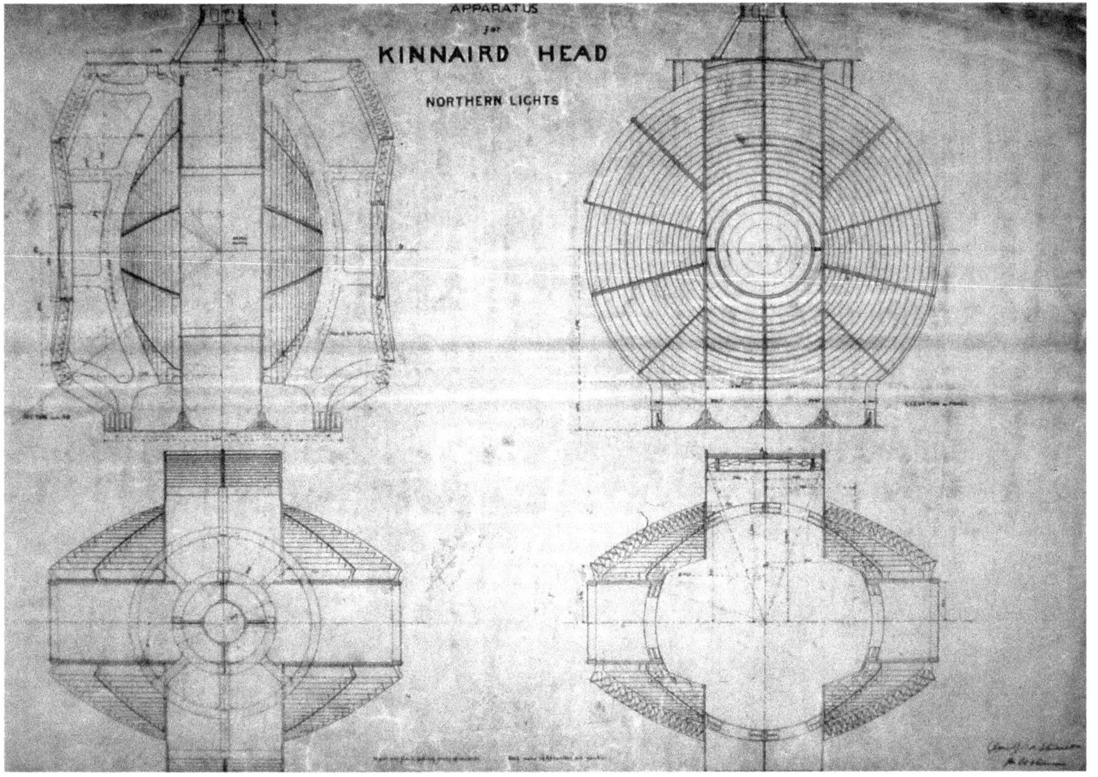

David's design for the new single-flash hyper-radial lens. Single-flash lenses were more powerful and efficient than group flashing lenses of the same size, and thus had a greater range. (Northern Lighthouse Board)

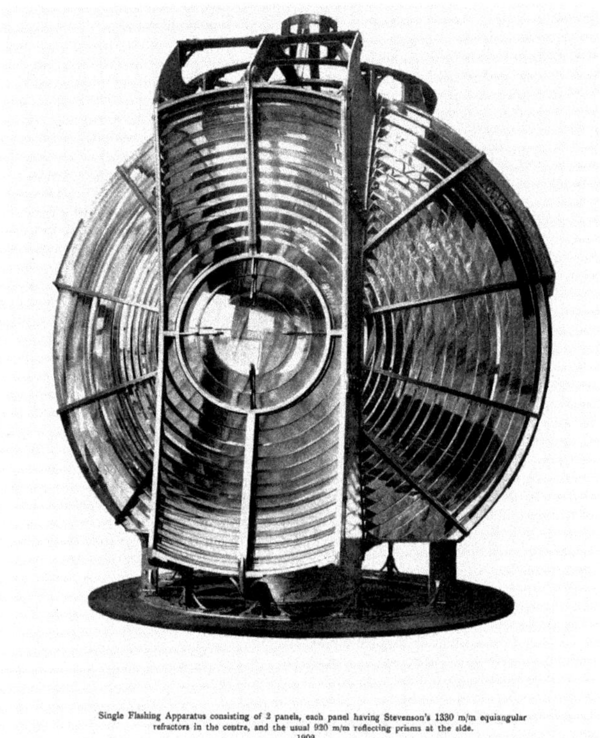

Kinnaird Head's lens photographed *c.* 1901 in the Chance Brother's factory, Smethwick near Birmingham, before being transported to Fraserburgh. (Collection of the Museum of Scottish Lighthouses, Fraserburgh)

exterior cast iron walls, each fabricated sheet having a single hole to cater for a new style of ventilation system, allowing for a supply of air to enter the light-room. These holes were capped on the inside by decorative brass stops, which would be opened or closed by the keepers on duty by turning them. Another new feature to the lantern dome was the weather vane, which doubled up as a chimney. The chimney tube began less than a metre above the paraffin lamp, allowing for most of the smoke and vapours to be drawn from the lamp. The genius of the design was by rotating with the weathervane, so the excess smoke was always taken down wind. This meant that it could not be blown back into the lantern as well as ensuring no freak gusts could endanger the light.

Key to the upgrade was not only the brilliancy of the light but also the introduction of a flashing light at the station. This meant the installation of clockwork machinery to rotate the huge lens to create a flash sequence. The lens sat on a turntable of twelve steel rollers with brass facings that were packed with steel ball-bearings each taking an equal burden of weight. When engaged onto the clockwork mechanism the lens was rotated by means of a dropping weight that was suspended directly beneath the machinery which descended down Stevenson's lighthouse tower. In order to allow for the continual rotation of the lens, the keepers would be required to wind the weight back to the top of the tower every half an hour. The machinery was made by the Dove Company of Edinburgh at a cost of £1,807 and was the most advanced of its time. Not only did it rotate the lens, it also pumped paraffin oil from a cistern on the floor to the new six wick lamp.

These improvements were effected in the closing months of 1902, the new light being operational from 5 January 1903. The flash character of the light was set at one

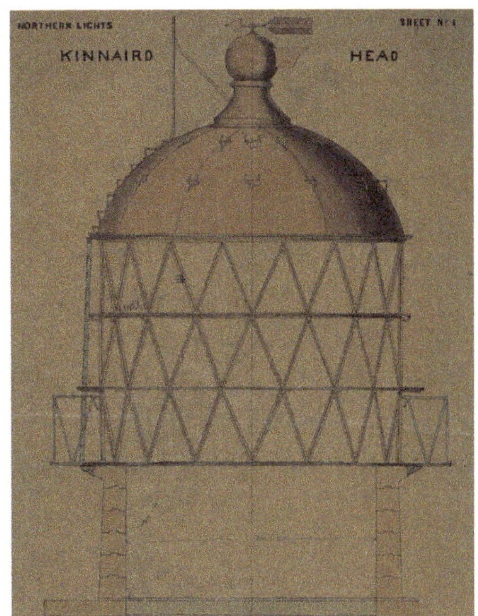

The lantern of 1902 was the fourth and last to be constructed for Kinnaird Head. Note the weather vane on top of the dome, which was part of the chimney. It allowed smoke to only be taken down-wind, and ensured no freak gusts extinguished the lamp. (Northern Lighthouse Board)

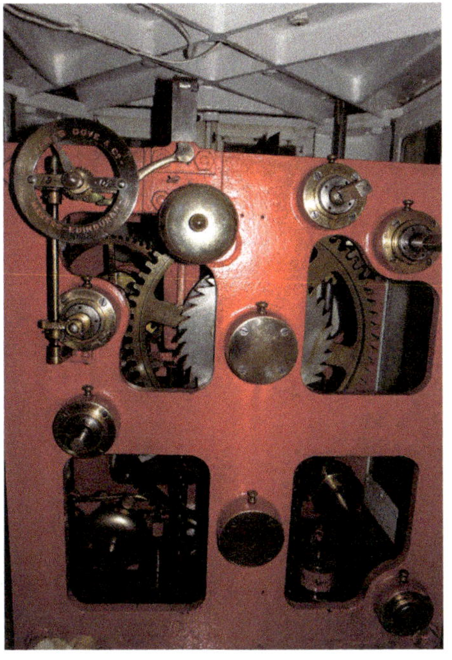

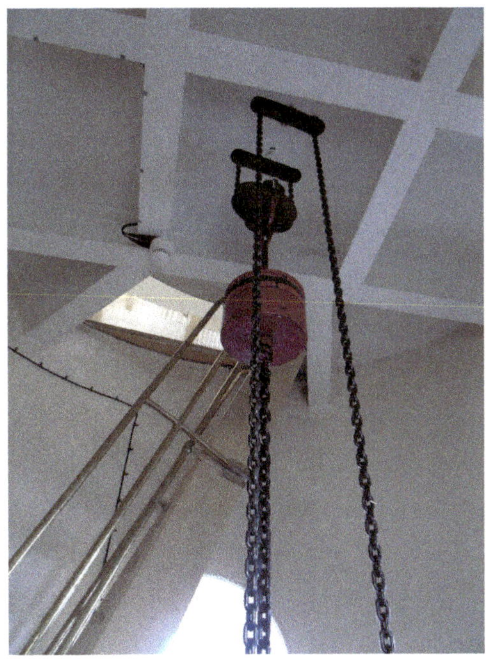

Above left: The lens was rotated by a clockwork machine, which in turn was driven by a dropping weight. The keepers had to wind the machine every half an hour to keep the lens rotating.

Above right: This weight pulled round the gears of the mechanism as it descended Stevenson's 1823 tower. The rotation of the lens had to be precise (one rotation every thirty seconds resulting in a flash every fifteen seconds) requiring slip weights to be added or removed from the main weight to adjust speed.

flash of white every 15 seconds, meaning the keepers had to ensure one rotation of the lens apparatus – which had two faces – every thirty seconds. The light had a brilliancy of 109,000 candlepower and could be seen upwards of twenty miles out to sea. It must be noted that this character had not been the original proposal of the Stevenson brothers, who first advanced the idea of a lens with a group flash of five for Kinnaird Head – but this was rejected by the Masters Brethren of Trinity House in favour of the aforementioned single-flash apparatus. They believed it to be too similar to the triple-flash apparatus of Rattray Head's lighthouse built in 1895, which had already rendered Kinnaird Head's red sector obsolete.

The changeover was smoothly presided over by experienced Principal Keeper John Gilmour, who had the task of training his keepers in the working of the new light apparatus – including his near seventy-year-old occasional keeper, shoemaker Alexander Ritchie. While there was no complaint from within the lighthouse, there were some complaints from the wider community. The light was described as 'sending a brilliant beam of light across the sea for a distance of 18 miles, and also playing fantastically like a search light upon the town and surrounding district. Although this was a benefit to mariners, it led to one local carter, John Watt, to complain that the flashing light 'is dangerous to horse traffic on the highways around Fraserburgh and seeing that several accidents have been caused thereby.' His petition against the apparent horse-frightening raised only twenty-four signatures, and the matter was dismissed!

This light was further enhanced in 1906 when the six-wick burner installed in 1902 was superseded by the new incandescent paraffin vapour burners. First experimented with in 1904 in Scotland, the Stevenson brothers found these lamps burned seven

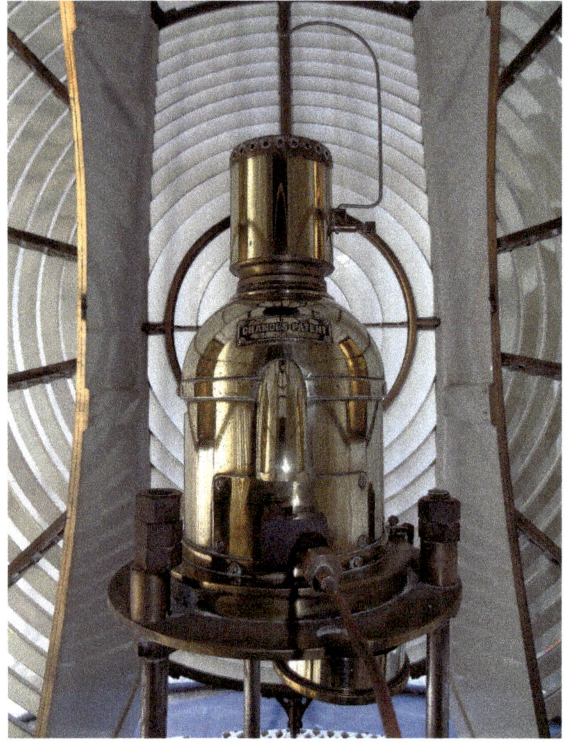

The 85 mm incandescent paraffin lamp sat on the pedestal within the hyper-radial lens. (Collection of Historic Environment Scotland)

times more brilliantly than the old wick lamps. They worked like an old tilly lamp, the paraffin being heated into a gas and burned off under a mantle. Kinnaird Head was given the 85 mm lamp – the largest size – which required the keeper to pressurise the paraffin tank via a handpump about every forty minutes. The lamp would burn through about 900 gallons of paraffin every year, all of which had to be carried to the top of the tower by the keepers in small paraffin flagons from the oil store. When the 85 mm incandescent lamp was used in conjunction with the hyper-radial lens it gave out 1,140,000 candlepower, which could be seen for as much as twenty-seven miles out to sea. As a consequence, according to David A. Stevenson in 1908, Kinnaird Head now exhibited the most powerful light in Scotland.

Foghorn

The lantern was not the only improvement underway at Kinnaird Head in 1902 as the Stevenson brothers also introduced a foghorn to the site. Foghorns were by no means a new technology in 1902 – just one that was slow to be introduced to Scotland due, in part, to a lack of interest by both the commissioners and the Stevensons. The foghorn, as they are recognised today, was the invention of the Scottish emigrant Robert Foulis (1796–1866) in the Canadian port of St John, New Brunswick, in 1853. His steam-power foghorn, giving out a low-pitched blast, was inspired by listening to his daughter playing the piano. When taking long walks, he noticed the low-pitched notes she played carried farther in the fog than the high notes. They were quick to develop across America, but it was not until 1876 that the first NLB foghorn was built at St Abb's Head in Berwickshire, powered by hot air and imported from America.

By the time Kinnaird Head's foghorn was built in 1903 they were a fairly common sound around the Scottish coast – particularly on the east coast where the thick summer haars led to them being almost constant annoyances. The residents of Fraserburgh would have been no stranger to the sound of foghorns, the distant blasts of the high-power

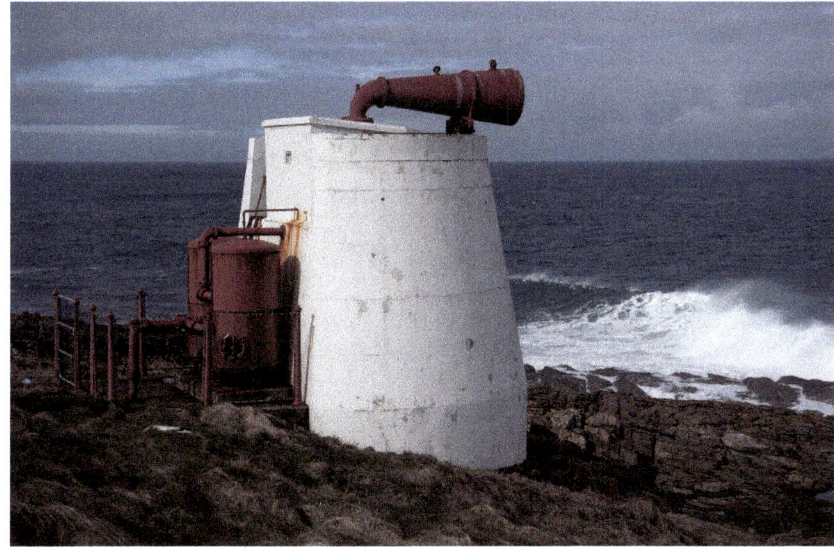

The foghorn, operational from 1903, was known locally as the 'Castle Coo' due to the low-pitched 'mooing' sound it created. (Billy Watson)

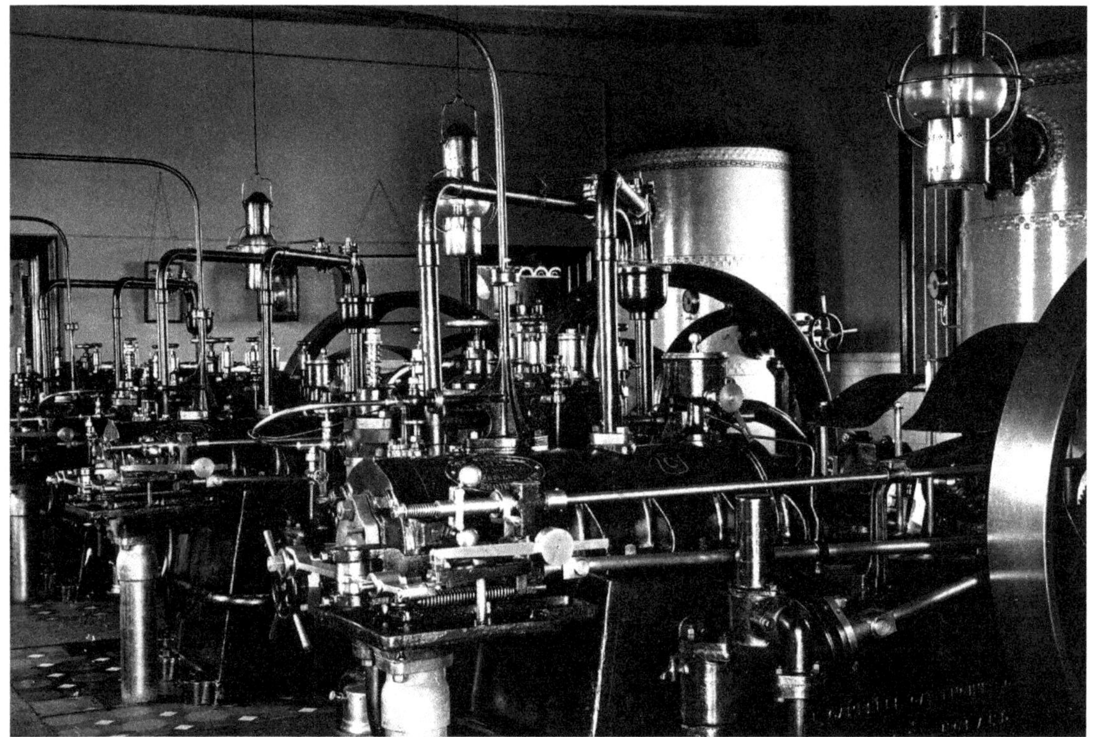

The foghorn originally operated using paraffin-driven Crossley engines with their noted flywheels. Crossleys were used at Kinnaird Head until 1950 when they were replaced with Kelvin-Diesel engines. (Quentin Stevenson Collection, Museum of Scottish Lighthouses)

Rattray Head siren being heard in the town from some twelve miles distance. Having a foghorn in their own back yard would be an entirely different experience. While the construction of the foghorn apparatus begun in late 1902, it would be November 1903 before it was completed and operational. It was a huge undertaking as not only was a twenty-four-foot concrete foghorn tower required, but also an enginehouse and a new keepers' cottage for the additional manpower required at the site. The building work alone, which was awarded to local firm Brebner & Jenkins, cost £3,000 with an additional £7,000 being spent on the mechanical aspects of the build.

The foghorn was powered by compressed air, for which three 20 hp paraffin-driven engines were required. While the horsepower may not have been great these engines were large and imposing. They were described as 'the latest and most improved pattern' as provided by the Manchester-based Crossley Brothers. They ran on the purest paraffin, which was heated and vaporised to a gas in order for the compressors to run. The engines could be started within seven minutes of the first sight of fog 'and once in motion they require a minimum of attention, stoking and other labour connected to the steam engines being disposed with.' This was key to their success as the engines may be required to power the horn for as long as twenty-four hours or more in the worst fogs. Compressed air was forced into air receivers before being conveyed to the horn itself in underground pipes. The first puff of air to reach the siren chest wound a weight on a clockwork machine which started a pendulum. Just as the lights flashed, the foghorns had regulated blast sequences.

At Kinnaird Head the horn would blast for seven seconds every minute and a half. David A. Stevenson decided the horn would be a low pitch, as he deduced that this would travel further than the two notes of different pitch desired by Trinity House. On this matter, Stevenson triumphed over the elder brethren! The clockwork would allow the compressed air to travel through a diaphone – or siren – which was located directly beneath the cast-iron horn. Being of high power, this horn is a full sixteen feet long and six feet in diameter at its widest part.

The completed foghorn apparatus was introduced to the people of Fraserburgh in the first week of November 1903. During its seventy-two-hour trial for the commissioners of Northern Lights, the *Fraserburgh Herald* reported that 'in the neighbourhood of the lighthouse the sound was deafening, and the vibration in the atmosphere very marked.' The harbourmaster received reports that the foghorn was heard 'very distinctly' seventeen miles at sea. While this may have been a shock to residents, it was one they would need to become accustomed to. The addition of the foghorn permanently changed personnel numbers at Kinnaird Head as a foghorn meant the station would require an additional keeper. With only two cottages existing on the site, part of the expense of the apparatus included the building of an extra cottage for this third keeper. It was slightly larger than the other two houses, and thus was swiftly taken by the Principal Keeper who was, on occasion, expected to host any NLB official staying at the station overnight. The house was built on the south side of the complex in the land where Mr Harvey's magnificent vegetable garden had formerly stood.

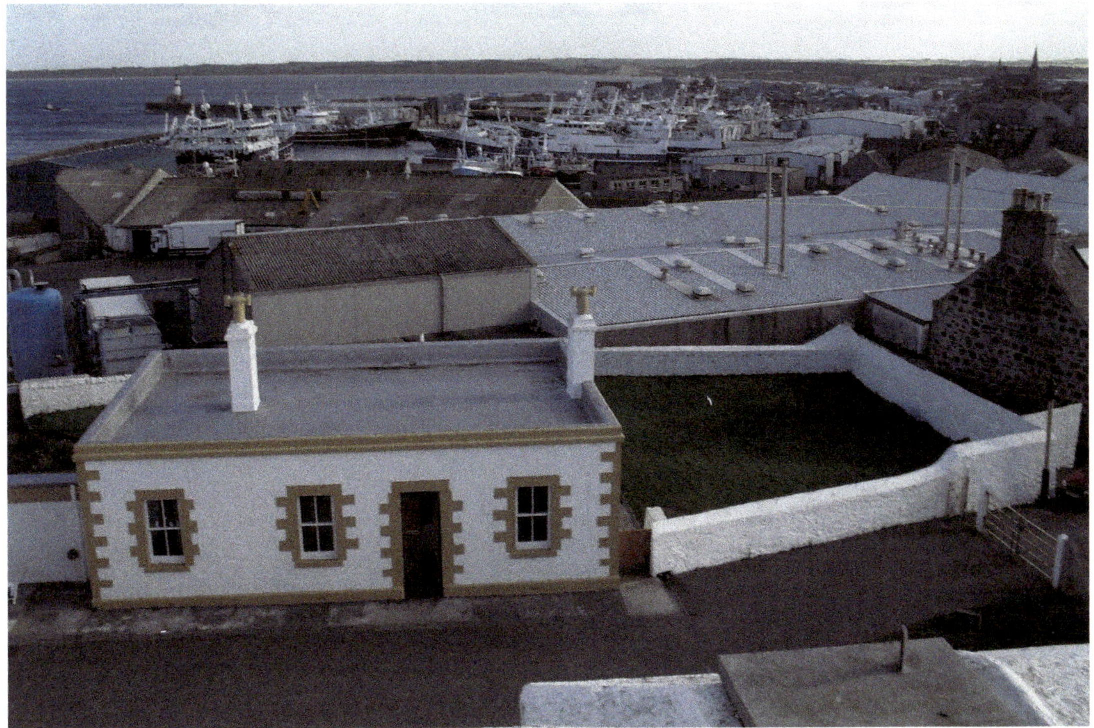

The costs of the foghorn included a new dwelling house for an additional keeper. The principal lightkeeper's cottage was built in 1902 partly on the land formerly taken up by Mr Harvey's garden!

Chapter 7

Last of the Stevensons

Minor Lights

While the works of 1902–04 undoubtedly improved navigation on the east coast there was one point – a mere two miles from Kinnaird Head – that continued to pose a threat to the mariner. Kinnaird Head's shipwreck register shows that between 1889 and 1904 the Cairnbulg Briggs claimed nine vessels out of a total twenty-two lost in the vicinity of the lighthouse. Following the improvements at Kinnaird Head, a further five vessels were lost on the Briggs in the period 1905–14.

This danger had to be addressed, the final straw coming in January 1912 when the Dundee-registered steam trawler *Clio* ran aground on the reef in bad weather. The Cairnbulg life-saving apparatus attempted a rescue but to no avail, causing the Fraserburgh lifeboat to be called out. The conditions, as well as the positioning of the stricken vessel, made the rescue difficult. The crew of the *Clio* were forced to abandon the vessel, tying themselves to the 1858 iron cage beacon. While this arguably removed them from immediate danger of death by drowning, Second Coxswain James Sim feared that if the men were left on the cage overnight most of them would die due to exposure by the morning. Sim and three other volunteers, eager to save life even when faced with

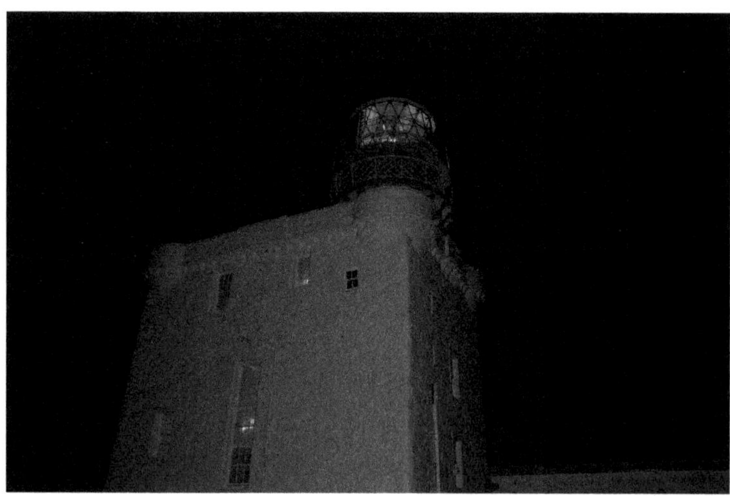

Sometime between 1902 and 1909 the keepers started lime-washing the tower as a day-marker. Note the elongated window on the south face of the tower, which was knocked through in 1902 for better access to the paraffin room: barrels could now be winched up on a pully, rather than small casks being carried up the spiral stairs.

great personal risk, swam out to the beacon with a line allowing the rescue to be effected. For such bravery Sim was eventually awarded the RNLI's bronze medal in 1929. Two bronze medals were awarded to volunteers of the Cairnbulg life-saving apparatus.

The cage beacon was proving an inadequate lifesaving measure for the new century, so a little over a week following the rescue, at a meeting of the Fraserburgh Harbour Commissioners, it was resolved that the Commissioners of Northern Lighthouses should be petitioned to 'provide a gas light on the beacon at Cairnbulg.' The fishermen were of the opinion that this would be extremely advantageous to seafarers, while Baillie Gordon of Fraserburgh stated: 'If there had been a light on the beacon the accident ... would never have occurred.' By November 1912 the NLB had confirmed they would undertake to establish a light on the reef, with work finally commencing in November 1913.

The works again fell to Engineer David A. Stevenson who, over the course of his tenure to the NLB, erected seventy-five automatic unmanned minor lights around Scotland. Building on the reef, which was covered during the high tide, was problematic, prompting Stevenson to build an unconventional structure. He was unable to build a solid pre-fabricated cast-iron tower as would be normal, so instead was forced to build his lantern on a twenty-seven-foot beacon structure similar to what was built in 1858. An AGA burner was placed in a beacon lantern – of the variety normally used

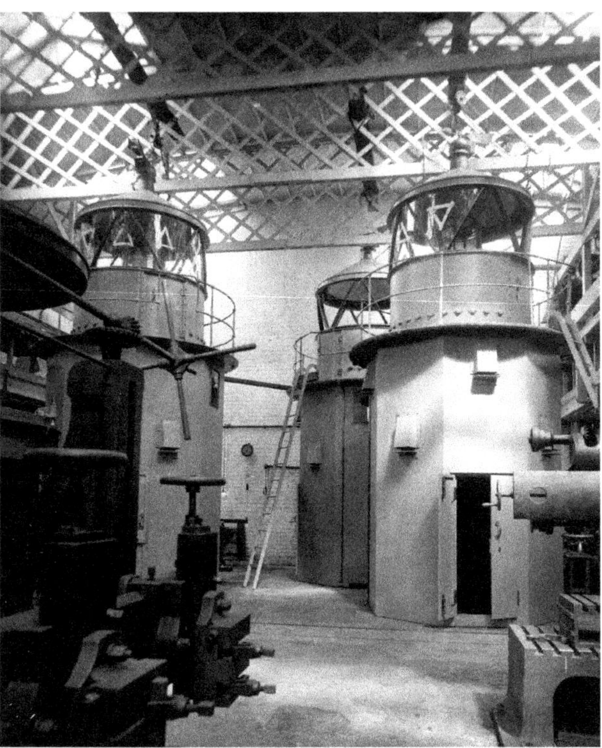

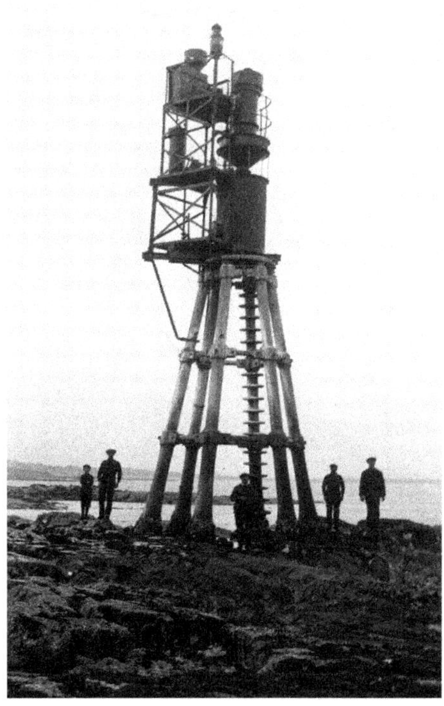

Above left: NLB standard, pre-fabricated, cast-iron minor lights sit in the Chance Factory *c.* 1910. (Quentin Stevenson Collection, Museum of Scottish Lighthouses)

Above right: Being built on a reef, the Cairnbulg beacon was constructed on a non-conventional cage tower. (Quentin Stevenson Collection, Museum of Scottish Lighthouses)

on buoys – which would separate the gas flow to burn a burst of gas as a flash. The acetylene gas was provided from tanks dug into the foot of the beacon. Another AGA invention – the sunvalve – would regulate the light, turning it on and off by the power of the sun. The device had a large central black rod, which expanded in sunlight to cut off the gas flow to the beacon and would retract in the darkness to re-establish gas flow. William Moyes Acetylene Company carried out the works installing the light and fog gun at a cost of £605. An attendant was appointed locally to check on this new beacon, but it was also observed from Kinnaird Head each night at midnight.

The marking of the Cairnbulg Briggs and the Rattray Briggs from 1895 made the north-east coast much safer for the mariner – marking a part of the coast which Kinnaird Head had historically failed to. Following 1918 a vessel would not strike the Cairnbulg point until 1925, with another accident not being reported on the Briggs until 1940. The beacon was first lit on 15 June 1914 giving a flash once every ten seconds, but its benefit would not be felt until four years later: war was declared on 4 August, and almost immediately this new light – along with all others – was purposely plunged into darkness.

The First World War

On 3 August 1914, as war with Germany ebbed closer, the British Foreign Secretary Sir Edward Grey uttered his famous quote about the coming conflict: 'The lamps are going out all over Europe, we shall not see them lit again in our life-time.' His prediction

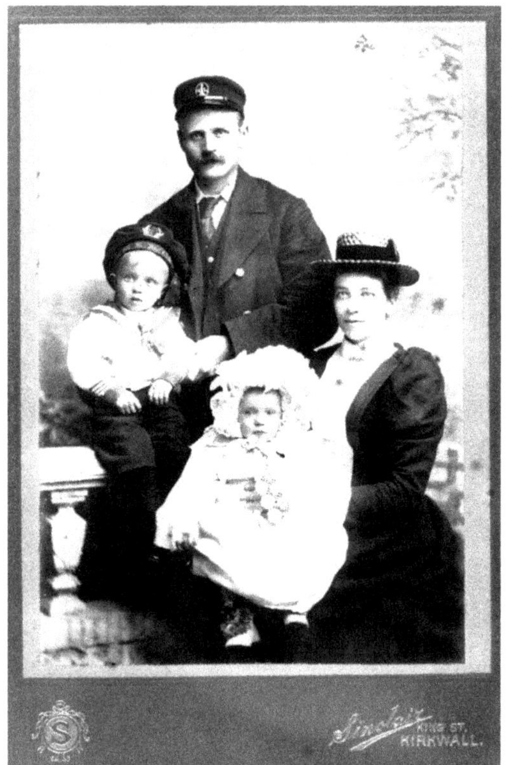

John Grant served as principal lightkeeper at Kinnaird Head between 1912 and 1919, taking in the duration of the First World War.

was certainly correct in its application to lighthouses as all were shut off, used only sparingly at the advice of the Admiralty. The fear was that German U-boats would use the lights at strategic targets for the accurate laying of sea mines. Kinnaird Head's position, on the extreme eastern point where the Moray Firth meets the North Sea, was particularly strategic with the risk of guiding enemy vessels into the Firth towards the important naval base at Cromarty.

John Grant, a paraffin oiler who had family connections to Fraserburgh, was serving as Principal Keeper when war was declared. Life at the station for him and his two assistants was relatively easy going, particularly compared to their neighbours at Rattray Head who had a near encounter with a zeppelin in May 1916. The light was extinguished for the duration of the war, the keepers only being required to continue with the regular duties of the foghorn as and when required. The light would, on occasion, be exhibited if it was requested by the Admiralty, used to guide warships through particularly precarious areas of the coast. This very seldom happened at Fraserburgh during the course of the First World War, but if it was required the keepers would be informed via a signalling station based somewhere in the grounds of Kinnaird Head. Not much is recorded about the signalling station other than it was operated by the Royal Naval Volunteer Reserve and it had armed personnel stationed there in Nissen huts. One man, Signalman Robert Fraser, was killed in July 1918 when a rifle accidentally discharged.

Mariners, particularly the fishermen, around the north-east coast found it difficult to safely navigate the coast during wartime. First there was the immediate issue of the war, which presented itself quite quickly in the seas around Kinnaird Head. As early as September 1914 one vessel had reported a sighting of a mine some 10½ miles from the lighthouse. This was received with reports of a German trawler being sighted flying a British flag. In May 1915 it was reported that another vessel had been pursued by a U-boat off Kinnaird Head, with two other trawlers being blown up. While all lights were extinguished to prevent advancing the enemy at sea, extinguished lights were also no use to civilian vessels.

There appears to have been few incidents caused by the coastal black out, one exception being the Peterhead-registered steamship *Pursuit*. In January 1915 the vessel was heading north from its home port when it was wrecked at near Rattray Head, according to one witness, 'on account of the leading lights not being lighted.' Bizarrely, rather than sailing well away from the rocky coastline the skipper decided 'to navigate the vessel chiefly by keeping within the sight of land.' The skipper relied on his local knowledge, but with no lights he mistook the Rattray Briggs for the Cairnbulg Briggs, altered his course, and lost his vessel. An inquiry blamed the skipper who was scalded for not showing more care 'knowing of the absence of coastal lights.' After four years of darkness, the reillumination of the coasts were welcomed by mariners with peace in 1918.

Wireless Beacon

Following the First World War the Stevenson engineers focussed their attention on the advancement of radio and wireless technologies. The Stevenson brothers were no strangers to radio communication with Charles A. Stevenson being a noted pioneer of radio signalling. Charles could claim to be an inventor of radio with his successful transmission of a signal over half a mile as early as 1892. This was even earlier than Marconi's experiments. Incidentally it may be a note of interest that Gugliemo

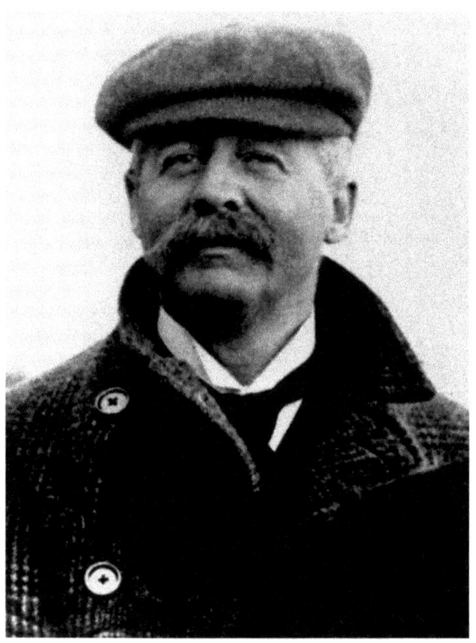

Although never appointed Engineer to the Northern Lighthouse Board, Charles A. Stevenson worked alongside his brother David and pioneered many technologies including wireless messaging.

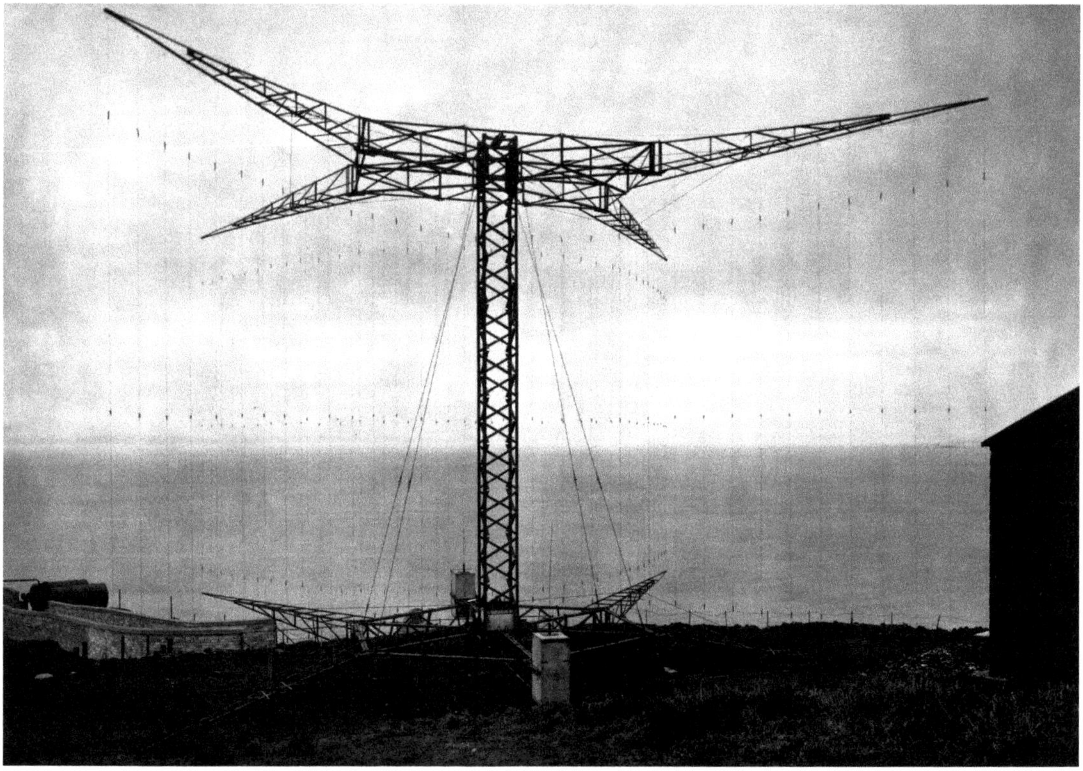

Between 1920 and 1925 the Marconi company trialled Wireless signalling from Inchkeith Lighthouse where this beacon was erected. The trials were successful and found to be useful for marine navigation. (Quentin Stevenson Collection, Museum of Scottish Lighthouses)

Marconi was no stranger to Kinnaird Head either as he had conducted successful radio experiments in the nearby village of Broadsea in 1904, less than a half mile from the lighthouse. Despite Charles' enthusiasm, history tells us that Marconi was the inventor of radio and as such it would be his company who would eventually serve the lighthouses. The Stevensons were keen on coded wireless transmissions, experiments at Inchkeith between 1920 and 1924 proving 'the system to be a valuable aid to navigation.'

Kinnaird Head was chosen as the site to host the Northern Lighthouse Board's first official radio beacon and by January 1929 a seventy-foot aerial mast was erected to the north of the lighthouse tower for transmitting signals. While work with the radio apparatus was undertaken by the Marconi Company, David A. Stevenson was still Engineer to the Board and he oversaw the whole operation including the building of a small stone-built room to house the transmitting apparatus. The wireless beacon at Kinnaird transmitted a signal in Morse code that could be picked up by passing mariners with wireless receivers. The code denoting the lighthouse was originally set as M. M. K. (or - - - - -.- in code) and was transmitted for sixty seconds in every four minutes, marking the lighthouse as a fixed point identifiable by direction finding equipment. These transmissions were sent twenty-four hours a day – day and night – and were intensified in foggy or 'thick' weather.

The new technology was widely welcomed by the mariners when the beacon officially started operating on 20 March 1929. One correspondent in the local *Press and Journal* newspaper wrote of its virtues: 'No human control is required: through daylight and darkness the messages fly automatically. Storms have no effect upon them.

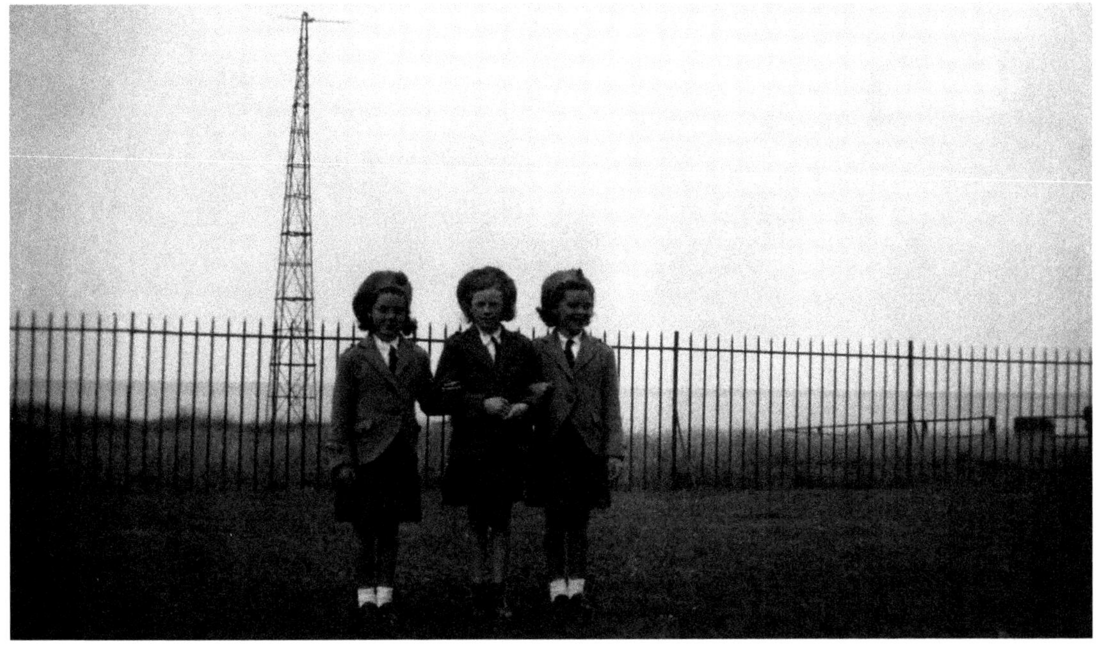

The Wireless beacon at Kinnaird Head was built to the north of Kinnaird Head Lighthouse in early 1929 and could reportedly send signals as far as 100 miles. It can be seen behind lighthouse children (left to right) Dorothy McLean, Mabel Campbell and Ishbel McLean *c.* 1943. (Reproduced by kind permission of Mabel Stewart)

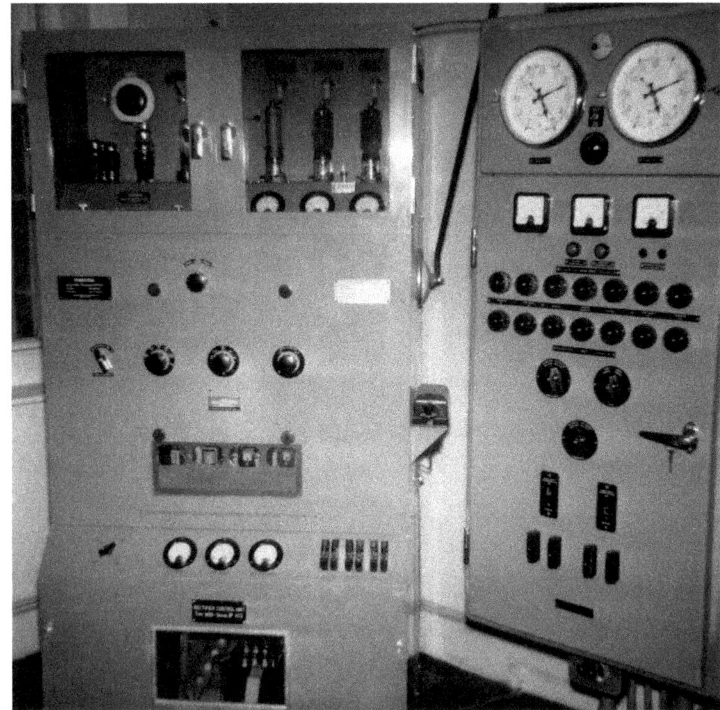

Inside the Radio Room
at Kinnaird Head,
1964. (Collection of
the Museum of Scottish
Lighthouses, Fraserburgh)

Fog, which can mask a lighthouse beacon or alter the apparent direction of blasts ... is powerless over the etheric waves.' He further described the radio room 'like being in a magic cave ... the master clock was set and the apparatus did the rest without the touch of human hand.' The beacon at Kinnaird Head had a range of 100 miles and was so successful that by 1937 six more had been built at lights around Scotland's coast.

Duncan McIntosh, who was taught how to operate the beacons at Kinnaird Head as a Supernumerary (Trainee) Keeper in 1964, has altogether different memories regarding the need of human assistance! The precise timing of the beacon's transmission was determined by a swinging pendulum which itself was driven by a dropping weight. This would slow down in colder weather with the effect that the keepers had to adjust it by placing cut quarters of old pennies onto the weight. Mr McIntosh also recalled that if the insulators at the base of the mast were showered in salt spray from the sea (which happened in stormy weather) it would reduce the strength of the signal. This was remedied by 'two keepers, one at the transmitter [room] and one at the mast base with a bucket of fresh water and a brush, would wash the insulators between transmissions.' If you are wondering why a keeper was required at the transmitter house, Mr McIntosh explains: 'The keeper at the transmitter would shout just before the next transmission to warn the other keeper ... this was to avoid electric shock, or possibly a fatal occurrence.'

The arrival of the wireless beacons brought the lighthouse service and navigational aids into a new age. It is perhaps fitting that this was the last technology the Stevenson dynasty introduced to Kinnaird Head lighthouse. When David A. Stevenson retired in 1938, it ended the Stevenson's 150-year service as Engineers to the Board. Starting with his blood great grandfather Thomas Smith, to his brother Charles, every member of that illustrious family had played their part and left their mark on the lighthouse at Kinnaird Head.

Chapter 8

The Lighthouse at War

The most serious disruption in the history of the Northern Lighthouse Board occurred during the years of the Second World War. The conflict would impact on every station in the service – land, island and rock – indiscriminately. When war came in 1939 it was of little surprise to most with military and civilian agencies – including the NLB – undertaking serious contingency planning in the months approaching the conflict.

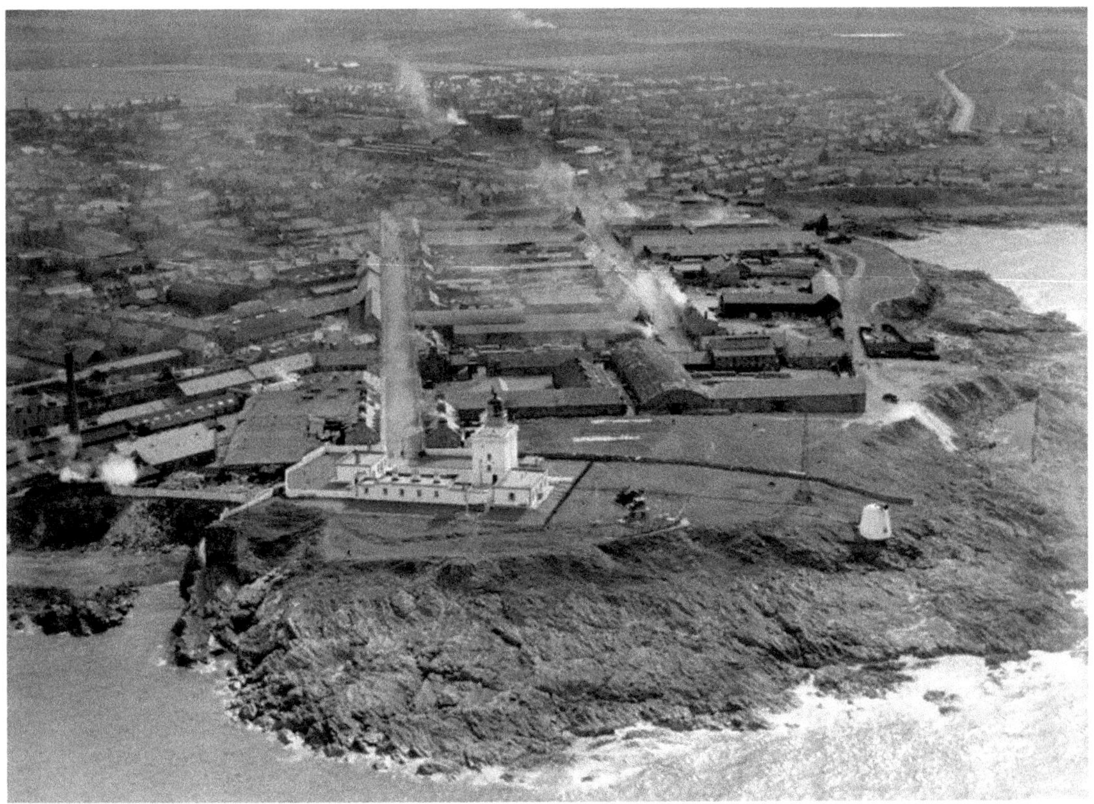

An aerial view of Fraserbugh in 1939. The keepers were instructed not to paint the tower during the war years to reduce its usefulness as a day marker for enemy aircraft.

The Board had begun drawing up its own response to war in April 1939, the bombing raids of the Spanish Civil War in 1936/37 serving as a warning of the full horror of total war and the potential of civilian targets and casualties.

Not only did the Board make plans regarding the operation of lights as it did during World War One, they were now also forced to make contingencies for the protection and safety of the keepers and families in their service and under their care in some of the most exposed and remote areas around the coast. On 9 May 1939 the Secretary to the NLB, J. Glencose Wakelin, sent a circular to all Principal Lightkeepers: 'The Commissioners are at present considering the question of Air Raid precautions in so far as the Lighthouse Service is concerned'. His letter tells of his belief, and that of the commissioners, that the risk of enemy aircraft attacking lighthouses 'is slight.'

Nonetheless, Principal Keepers were asked to reply informing of 'certain precautions' necessary at their stations. At Kinnaird Head the serving Principal, James G. McGaw, replied three days later noting little concern regarding his station.

McGaw informed Wakelin that there was no part of the station that would be suitable for a shelter, but confirmed that all the keepers and their families had already been measured by the local authorities for the size of gas mask they would require. He concluded his letter: 'As regards any special precautions being taken at the station we can see none, as you say the risk of being attacked by enemy aircraft is very slight – at a Lighthouse station.' It is clear from Wakelin's other correspondence that other Principal Keepers were not as relaxed as McGaw. The Secretary wrote to the Board of Trade: 'Several of them [keepers] have expressed concern regarding their vulnerability (perhaps somewhat exaggerated), and various suggestions have been put forward', such as reinforced concrete cellars.

While overseeing these measures for the keepers, Wakelin was also forming plans for the wartime operation of lights. A letter had been sent to the Principal Keepers in April 1939. This top secret letter contained a second sealed letter, with a note explaining the sealed letter 'is to be opened by you if and when you receive the following telegram from the Admiralty: 'Institute Phase IA'. The letters were kept in a 'lockfast place' and their contents were only to be known by the Principal and his assistants. With the outbreak of hostilities the keepers would eventually learn what Phase IA meant: 'I have now to instruct you as follows: Light to be extinguished forthwith.'

Wartime Operations at Kinnaird Head

On 1 July 1940 Assistant Keeper James Campbell, his wife, and young family arrived at their new home at Kinnaird Head lighthouse. This transfer was caused directly by the conflict, as when war was declared Campbell was the serving assistant at the Bass Rock lighthouse in the Firth of Forth. That light was abandoned by the NLB for the duration of the war because of its perilous position. Due to the fortifications of Leith and Granton the entire area around the light was now a minefield making it impossible to supply and therefore man. After a brief stint as a temporary keeper at Inchkeith, the Campbells were sent north to Fraserburgh.

By the time they arrived that summer Kinnaird Head was already under strict wartime operation. While the automatic minor light at Cairnbulg was extinguished in early September 1939, the major manned lights remained under normal operation until

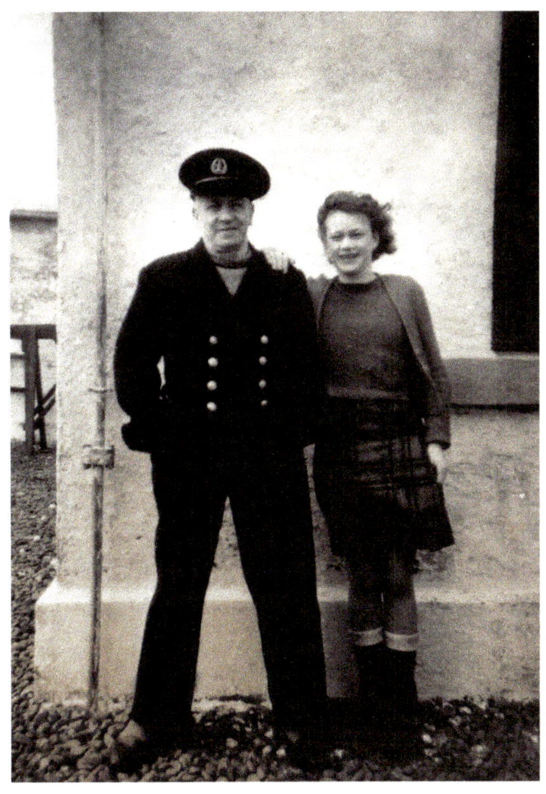

Assistant lightkeeper James Campbell with his daughter Mabel. (Reproduced by kind permission of Mabel Stewart)

December when Admiralty interference started to creep in. The light was ordered to be extinguished on 13 September between 15.50 and 22.35 hours. This remained the only order until 8 June 1940 when a Rear-Admiral at Invergordon ordered that the light was to be extinguished until further notice: it remained extinguished until 9 August. The light at Rattray was extinguished for most of the same period. The extinguishing of the light coincided with the fall of Norway and as the threat of indiscriminate civilian bombing was beginning to grow. The first Air Raid in Fraserburgh occurred on 16 July 1940, when three bombs were dropped on the town injuring thirty-six townspeople.

While the light was out during that raid, from mid-August the keepers were instructed to exhibit it at certain times as commanded by the Admiralty. As Mabel Stewart, daughter of James Campbell, recalled:

> The Admiralty would inform the Coastguard Station, situated next to the lighthouse, when the light was to be displayed. These were hours at which a convoy would be passing, usually around two hours. During the war years, ships sailed in convoys and would number from 30 to 100 ships.

Convoys would pass the light regularly, Mrs Stewart recalling watching the convoys being attacked by enemy aircraft 'with much flashing and gunfire'.

With hindsight Mr McGaw's letter to the Secretary in April 1939 failed to take seriously the threat posed by enemy aircraft. One issue he failed to take account of was the fact the lighthouse was situated next door to Maconochie's Kinnaird Head Works,

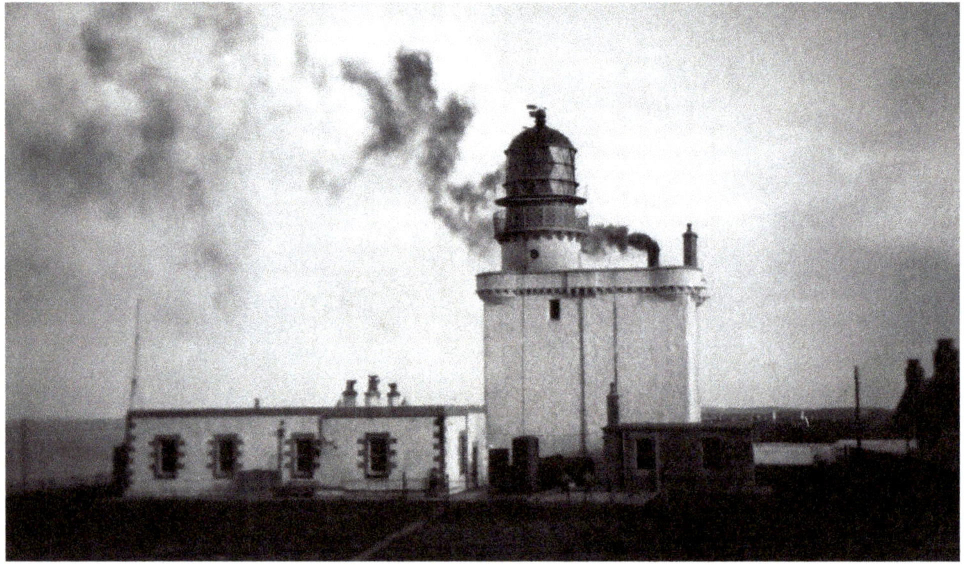

Picture of Kinnaird Head taken during the Second World War from the radio beacon *c.* 1941. Note the soot coming from Maconochie's factory. (Reproduced by kind permission of Mabel Stewart)

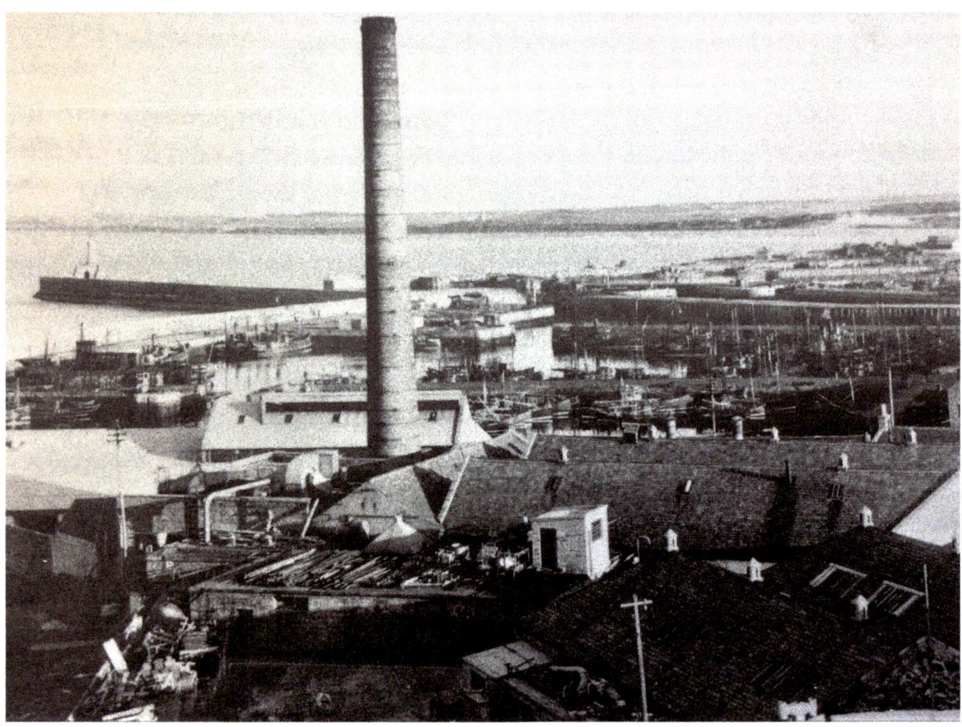

Maconochie's factory was targeted by the Luftwaffe during the Second World War. Its position, just over the lighthouse boundary wall, put the lighthouse at risk. The factory is pictured here from the lighthouse roof.

a canned food factory that would provide tinned rations to overseas troops. The town also had the Consolidated Pneumatic Toolworks, which operated as a munitions factory during the war. These two factors alone made Fraserburgh a target and, after the fall of Norway, one that would be increasingly targeted by low-flying 'hit and run' aircraft. Indeed, by the end of the war the town was known as 'Little London' due to the number of bombs dropped. It is not believed that the lighthouse was an intended target itself: it was just in the wrong place.

Mrs Stewart recalls that early on the keepers and families would take refuge in the coal store, referred to as the castle dungeon at the bottom of the lighthouse: 'We would shelter here armed with rugs and blankets, flasks of tea and sandwiches etc. We felt very safe. This was until it was pointed out that on the floor above the dungeon was where all the fuel for the lighthouse was stored and would be a death trap if it were to receive a direct hit.' After this realisation, the families used Morrison shelters provided by the NLB: practically a cage in which you would lay down inside your dwelling until the air threat had passed.

The controlled return of the light from August 1940 was not exactly welcomed locally: 'The keepers at Kinnaird Head were not very popular with locals when the flashing light came on piercing the darkness', Mabel recalls. The exhibiting of the light was becoming more frequent and by September 1940 the keepers had been instructed to show a light for five minutes on the hour and half hour. This would become a common signature, along with continual lighting for periods of passing convoys, for the duration of the war. As the attacks against Fraserburgh increased, so did paranoia that the light was to blame for these night attacks. On 13 November 1940 Provost Thompson of Fraserburgh wrote a complaint on behalf of the town regarding the light: 'In view of the

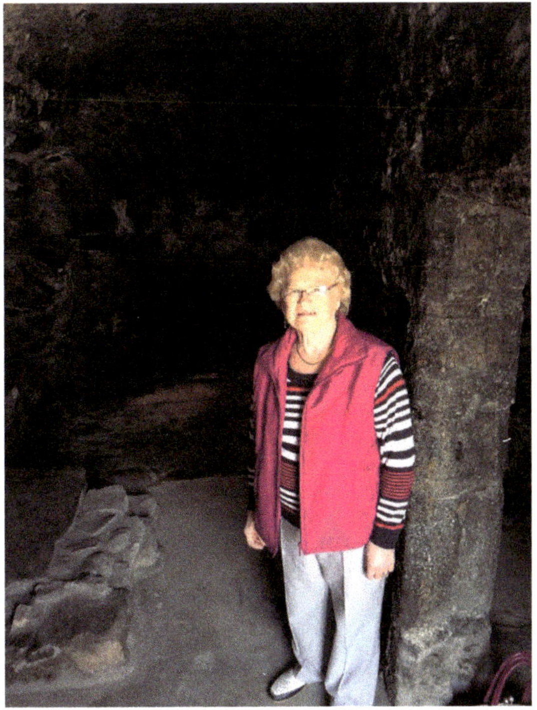

In 2016 Mabel Stewart, daughter of James Campbell, visited the 'dungeon' (lighthouse coal store), that the lightkeepers initially used as an air raid shelter.

necessity of enforcing a very strict blackout on the public the brilliant flash of Kinnaird over the town is causing considerable concern and even alarm.' The letter claimed that the light continued 'even during Air Raid warnings' and further advised 'that it would be practicable to shield the light between the West and South points of the compass, and that by doing so the town would remain in darkness.'

Provost Thompson's letter was sent only a week after a tragic bombing raid on the town centre on 5 November. There had been a fire at the Benzie & Miller's department store that evening, guiding the aircraft to drop bombs in the heart of the town. The Commercial Bar was hit, killing thirty-four people and injuring fifty-two. While the lighthouse was not to blame, its brilliant light clearly had people concerned. Would enemy aircraft follow the light just as it had followed the glare of the fire? To subdue these fears 'the greater part of the lantern' was painted black to limit the range of the light in accordance with Provost Thompson's wishes. In any case, the light was never exhibited during an air raid warning: that would cancel any Admiralty order. The station returns for November 1940 show careful notes to the following effect: '3rd, Light cancelled owing to Air Raid warning, no light shown between 6.35 + 9PM. 5th, No light between 7.30PM + 10PM Air Raid.'

Attacks and Defence

While Kinnaird Head was never a primary target of the Luftwaffe during the war, Maconochie's factory was obviously of interest to the 'hit and run' aircraft passing over Fraserburgh. In February 1941 it was the intended target of a bombing raid by a now familiar low-flying aircraft that dropped two 1000 lb bombs in the vicinity. One bomb landed on Castle Terrace, the street leading to the lighthouse gates, destroying houses, while the second hit the factory grounds. Thankfully on this occasion only fifteen people were injured, but the force of the blasts was enough to cause damage to the lighthouse.

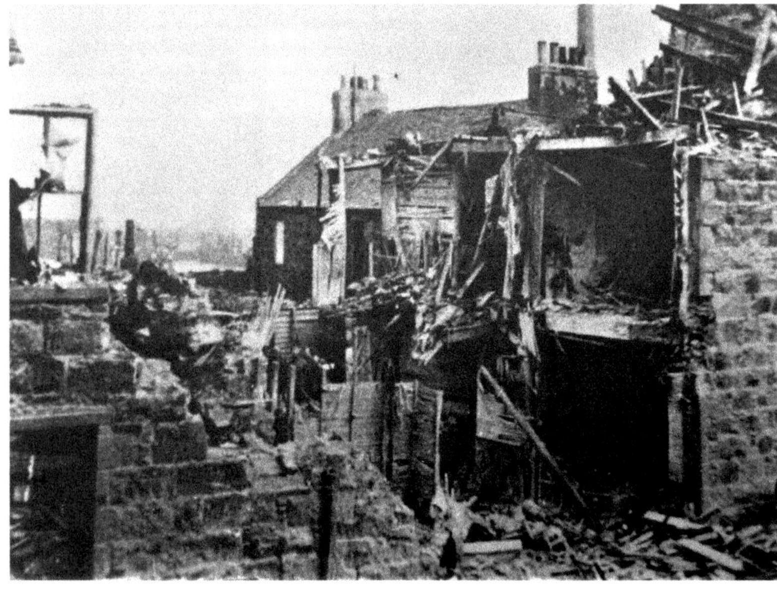

Bomb damage to Castle Street, close to the lighthouse 1941.

It was reported that: '3 lantern panes destroyed, the Radio Beacon aerial cut and several insulators broke, 41 panes of glass in the dwelling houses broken and frames damaged, 1 sliding bolt on the balcony door broken. The Supernumerary keeper's Room ceiling was cracked, and the ceiling of the first assistant's kitchen was cracked.' Less than two months later there was a second attack where two 500 lb bombs were dropped, causing six fatalities at Maconochie's factory.

Despite this, the only permanent damage to the station, still present today, can be noted on the hyper-radial lens. For many years a story passed down through the keepers telling that the damage to the lens was caused by bullets during the Second World War. The author – due to the absence of any written documentary evidence – had reached the conclusion it was nothing more than a story, particularly after seeing what machine guns had done to the Rattray lens. His opinion was changed after first meeting Mabel Stewart in the lightroom who gave her account: 'I heard the sound of a plane approaching, and machine gun fire. I ran out of the house to get to the "dungeon". Bullets fell around me. It was at this time that a bullet hit one of the lenses in the lighthouse lantern.'

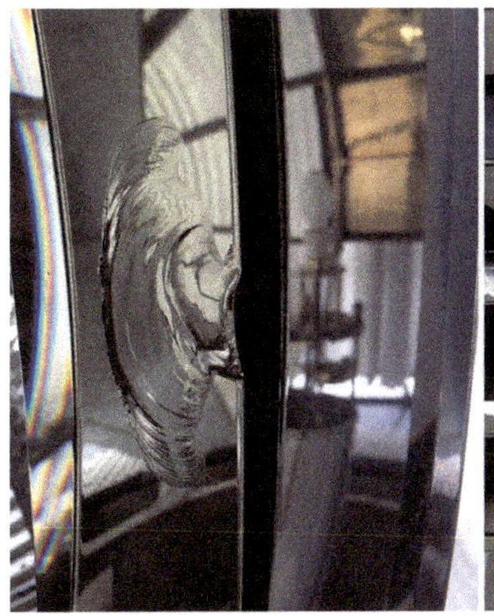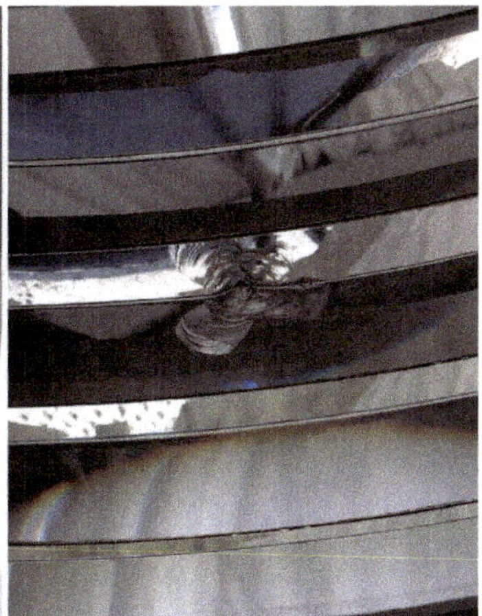

Kinnaird Head's hyper-radial lens sustained minor damage during the war due to stray bullets being fired by low-flying aircraft.

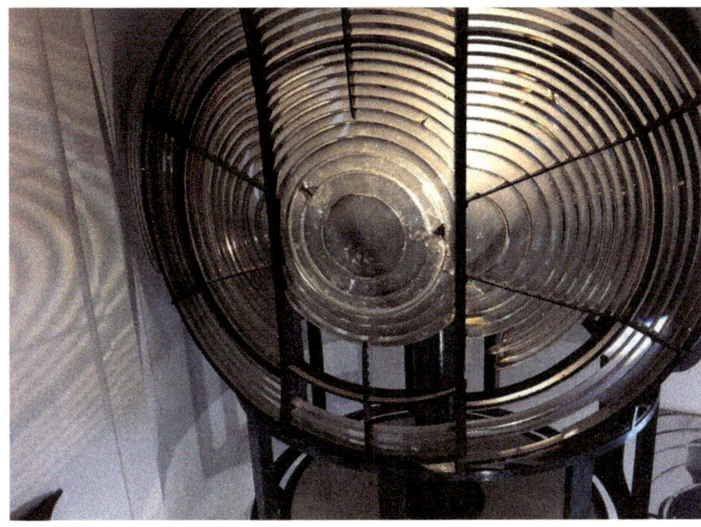

The Rattray Head lens, now on display at Aberdeen Maritime Museum, suffered more serious damage due to machine-gunning during the war. (Courtesy of Aberdeen Art Gallery and Museums, Aberdeen City Council)

Although it seems likely that the hit to the lighthouse was collateral from an attack on the factory the Board's earlier assumptions that lighthouses would not be targeted were quickly proven to be wrong. Various lights across the east coast in particular had been attacked – mainly by machine-gun fire. This led to the NLB to consider – and ultimately executing – a scheme of arming the lighthouses for defence purposes. While the Bell Rock and Rattray Head were armed, Kinnaird Head was not – meaning that the keepers did not man the guns. It was, nonetheless, a militarised zone utilised for the purposes of defence. First, in August 1940 a pillbox was built to the east side of the tower (beside the Wine Tower) and then in October the Principal Keeper reported to Edinburgh: 'I have to inform you that work commenced in connection with the erection of Lewis Guns, on the flat roof outside the Lighthouse tower.' Within a fortnight the promontory was garrisoned, with Nissen huts being built on the greens surrounding the lighthouse – presumably for the personnel who were to man the guns. It is not recorded if these guns were ever used in anger. The only physical evidence that they existed found at the lighthouse today are the empty ammunition boxes, kept by the thrifty keepers as storage containers. The guns were on site for about one year, being removed in October 1942.

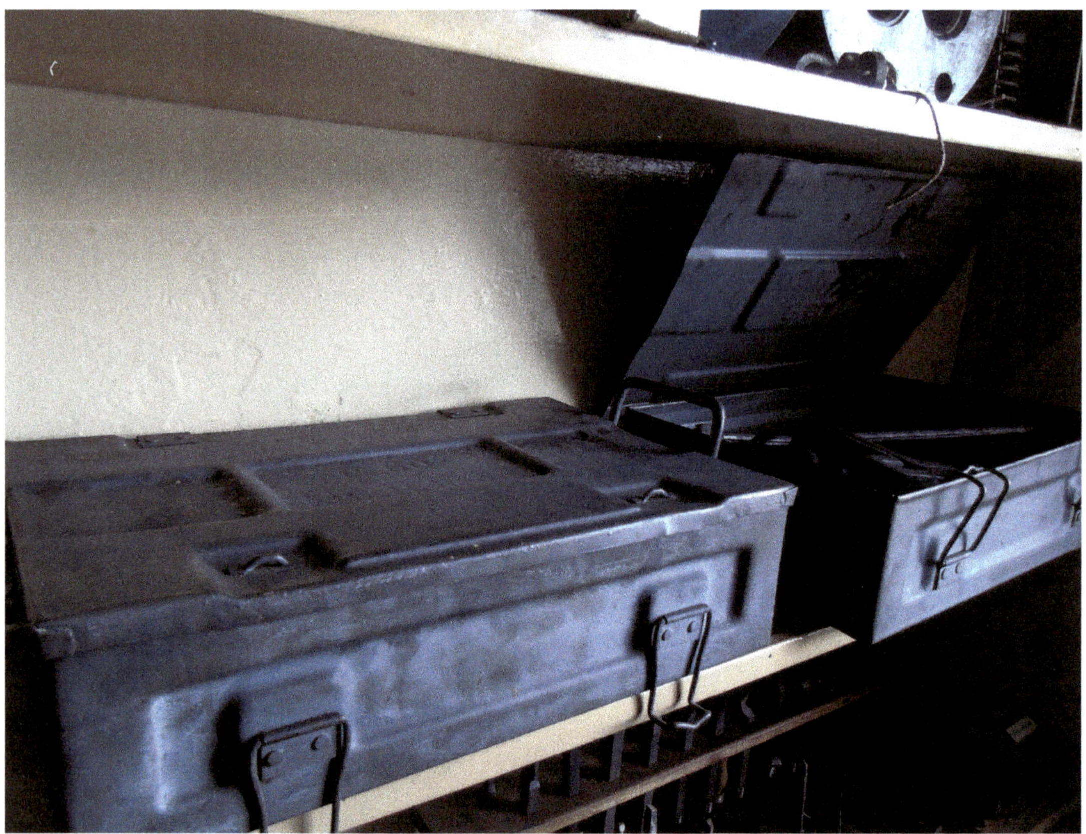

Today four ammunition boxes, retained by the lightkeepers as storage boxes, are the only evidence of the guns once placed on the roof at the lighthouse. (Collection of Historic Environment Scotland)

Other Notable Events

Principal Keeper James G. McGaw, who had served twelve years at Fraserburgh, received his orders to proceed to his new posting at Ailsa Craig on 16 March 1942. He was replaced by Alexander MacLean who brought a young family with him to Kinnaird Head, including twin daughters Ishbel and Dorothy. Six months older than Mabel, the three would become 'special friends'. Just over a month after arriving at the station Mr McLean had to deal with a bizarre occurrence. He reported to the Secretary that on 20 April 1942 Mr Campbell, 1st Assistant, had found a girl aged about nineteen years of age lying sleeping under the ladder leading to the lightroom on his way to take watch: 'The light was burning full brilliancy at the time and on waking her up she was apparently suffering from loss of memory.' Mabel recalls her father finding the girl: 'It was obvious to him, when he spoke to her, that she was unwell and couldn't tell him who she was or where she had come from. He brought her down to our house and in the morning the Doctor and then the police were sent for. She was taken away by the police and we never saw her again.' Being the war years, coupled with her loss of memory and refusal to give her name, this led to some suspicions at the lighthouse. For many years the occasional keeper, Mr Buchan, told the story to his family of his belief that the girl was a German spy! In truth she was an English Land Army Girl who had cycled from St Fergus, presumably following the brilliant light.

In February 1943 the Hydrographic Department complained to the NLB that on 11 January the light at Kinnaird Head 'was showing 1½ seconds short of its proper period'. As written earlier, displaying a false character was the worst offence a keeper could commit, and if the charge was proven a keeper would be dismissed. In his report to the commissioners, the Principal Keeper told that he and both assistants had tested the machine and found the 'timing was practically perfect'. If the character was indeed wrong, it may have been caused by the chaotic nature of wartime operations, starting and stopping the machine. It may also have been caused by cold weather, which could thicken lubricants and slow down the lens: 'Most of the machines are somewhat sensitive to weather conditions in the winter time and need slight increases or decreases in weight as may be necessary.' At any rate the Board found no fault with any of three keepers, and as such no action was taken against them.

On 10 December 1943 James Campbell received his promotion to become Principal Keeper. He would be sent to Skerryvore and the family sent to live at the shore station at Erraid. 'I still have many happy memories of Kinnaird Head', says Mabel. 'Of learning to ride a bicycle on the courtyard in front of the houses. Time spent on the six-hole putting green that my father had made on the strip of grass inside the front gate, of flying kites and playing on the rocks in front of the lighthouse and so much more.' A new keeper arrived to replace the Campbells in due course with the wartime operations continuing at Kinnaird Head for another year and a half.

Chapter 9

The Last Lightkeepers

Following the war one constant at Kinnaird, as at every other lighthouse in Scotland, was the continual transfer of keepers after about four or five years of service; a process that only ended with automation. No official reason was ever given for this system of periodic transfers, but it is generally accepted it was seen to be the fairest deal for the lighthouse families. Not only were keepers paid by length of service rather than difficulty of location (bar a small rock allowance) but the families had to move when the keepers moved, regardless of how remote or desolate their new locations. In the case of rocks, keepers would be separated from their family for six or more weeks at a time. All this meant that Kinnaird Head was a very welcome posting and one that was more conducive to a normal family life.

In August 1948 Assistant Lightkeeper Alastair Hislop arrived at Kinnaird Head following a six-year posting at the Bell Rock lighthouse, regarded as one of the most cramped and claustrophobic in the service. He remarked of his new station: 'It's a welcome change. Six years is a long time to be on the Inchcape Rock.' While at Kinnaird Head Hislop served alongside Assistant Keeper Charles Mathieson who, similar to him, had a young family. In July 1951 Mathieson, then the most senior assistant in Scotland, received orders that he was to be promoted to the rank of Principal Keeper, but as Kinnaird Head already had a Principal, Mathieson and his family would have to be transferred. The celebration of his promotion was short-lived as the family duly received orders that they would be sent to Fair Isle South lighthouse.

The Fair Isle lights were not the worst of stations but their location, on either end of an island between Orkney and Shetland supporting a population of about 70–100, was not ideal for a young family. The commissioners found this out to their peril when they arrived at Kinnaird the following month after encountering Mrs Mathieson! The story is recounted in Commissioner Sir Randall Philip's diary: 'The lighthouse keepers [at Kinnaird Head] all had families and rejoiced in the chance to send their children to the Fraserburgh schools. One mother [Mrs Mathieson], with five children, was upset at being informed that her husband was to move to Fair Isle. She evidently had a scene with Glen (Secretary to the NLB).' These transfers often hit the wives and children the hardest, the experiences in both 1948 and 1951 highlighting Kinnaird Head's desirability among the Scottish lights.

Regardless of the type of station, the transfer process was always undoubtedly an unwelcome upheaval for families. Part of the issue was that keepers never really knew

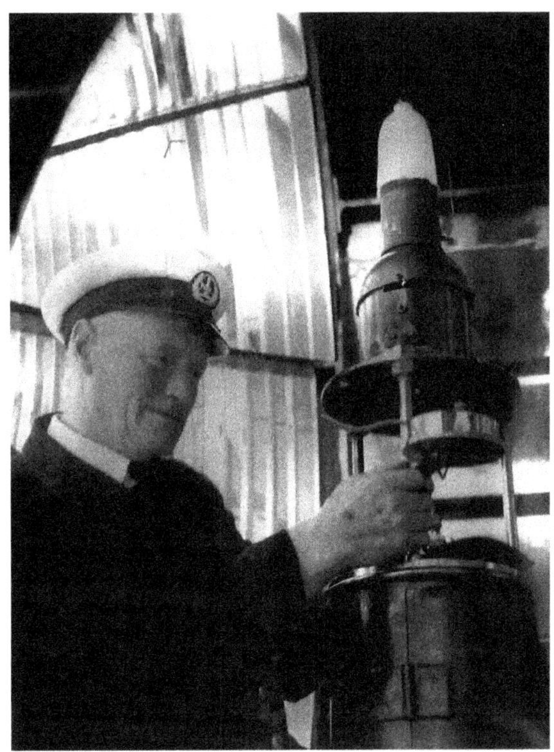

John R. Scott, principal keeper 1957–64, lights the paraffin lamp that was still being used into the second half of the twentieth century. (Reproduced by kind permission of Sydney Scott)

how long they would be at a station before being moved. It could be one year; it could be ten years. When the orders were received, they were usually given three weeks to a month's notice before being moved. When John R. Scott was transferred to Kinnaird Head from Dunnet Head in November 1957 he was given just eighteen days' notice. His son Sidney remembers the experience well: 'All belongings, furniture, bedding, crockery, toys, household goods – everything – had to be packed in boxes and then crated for transfer by many different means of transport.' As well as moving belongings, children would also have to move school which Mr Scott recalls was 'always a disruptive problem.'

When the Petries arrived at the station in 1965 they were sorry to leave their former station behind. Albert may have been serving at Inchkeith – a rock station – but the family accommodation was in Edinburgh! This was, therefore, one of those rare situations where Kinnaird Head was a downgrade! While Mrs Janet Petrie noted the benefits of the amenities of Fraserburgh (her son Brian could walk to school), her enduring memory of Fraserburgh was the overpowering smell of fish from the 'gut factory' and the annoyance of 'dirty sooty stuff' that fell from the loom of the nearby factory, dirtying clean washing on the line. As well as having neighbouring houses, Kinnaird Head was surrounded by industry.

As the world modernised in the 1960s, the old formalities continued at the lighthouse. There was still an order of precedence that had to be observed at the station. Mrs Petrie recalled: 'We always addressed the Principal as Mr Gifford. It was the Principal and Mrs Gifford ... unless they asked you to use their first name and that was very seldom done in the early days.' Even the Principal's wife had her place in the pecking order: 'They didn't rule over you, but they let you know they were the Principal's wife.'

After three years the Petries were sent to the Flannan Isles and oversaw that light's change to automatic. On moving, Mrs Petrie took a practical view: 'It was your work and you had to accept it, but [I was] concerned about my son's schooling.'

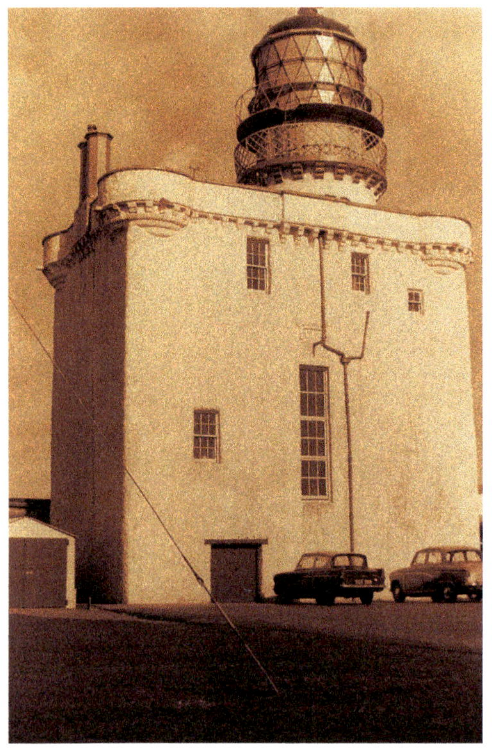

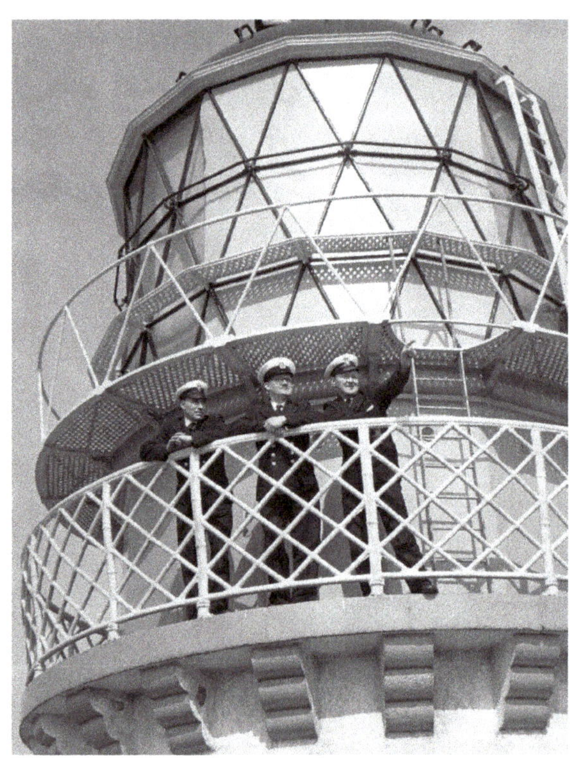

Above left: Kinnaird Head Lighthouse *c.* 1960.

Above right: Assistant keeper James Hunter, Principal keeper William Gifford and assistant keeper Albert Petrie on the balcony at Kinnaird Head *c.* 1966. (Reproduced by kind permission of the Petrie family)

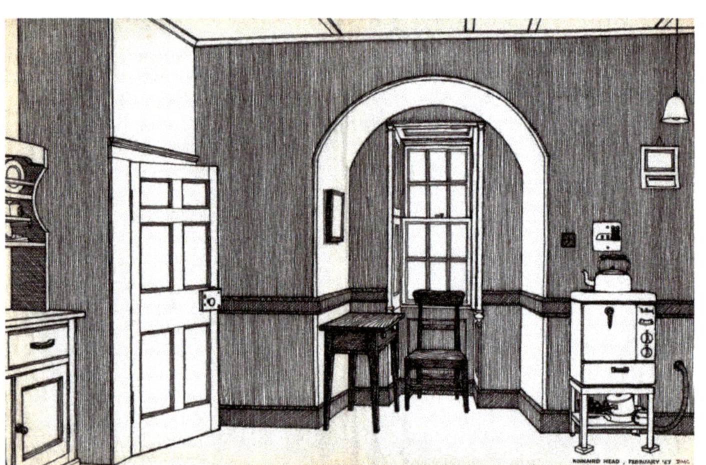

Ink drawing of the supernumerary quarters, by training keeper D. Cameron, 1967. (Dee Cameron Collection, Museum of Scottish Lighthouses)

In Kinnaird Head's order of precedence there was almost always the most junior of all keepers: a Supernumerary (trainee). As a fairly easy-going station it was a designated training station where keepers would get their initial instruction for about six weeks before being moved on to other, more challenging lights. The old castle tower provided extra rooms at the station that were used as a so-called bothy to house the Supernumerary. Mr Jim Aiken was sent to Kinnaird for training in December 1954, his wife Margaret describing his room in her book *Twelve Light Years* some years later: 'It was a large, grey room with a huge, black range in the fireplace and a small bed bought or made to fit into an alcove. Jimmy (five-feet ten-inches tall) had to lie diagonally to fit into it.' The couple were officially engaged in that room and spoke to the Principal Keeper Mr Firth and his wife about their hope of not being posted to a rock that would see them separated. Mr Firth's advice: 'If it is a rock, remember that there's always the homecoming.' Duncan McIntosh arrived as a Supernumerary in 1964 as 'Lord of the Manor living in a castle', much improved from his accommodation at Corsewall: 'a converted store which was shared by the occasional keeper.'

Approaching Automation

By 1970 the Northern Lighthouse Board's policy of full-scale automation was beginning to intensify. As the Engineer to the NLB, J. W. Williamson, himself noted in an internal memo in 1973, 'The NLB is embarked on a programme whereby within the next decade a considerable number of stations will become fully automatic.' Interestingly, in this age of modernisation, it was being noted by the keepers that Kinnaird Head was lagging behind in this drive. On his arrival at the station in 1973 Principal Keeper Magnus McDonald seemed puzzled as to why the station was still operating a paraffin lamp: 'It is a great pity that electricity cannot be used when the station has such a good supply of.' It was baffling; the height of the tower was illuminated by electric lighting yet for the want of an extra five metres of cable it did not extend to the lightroom.

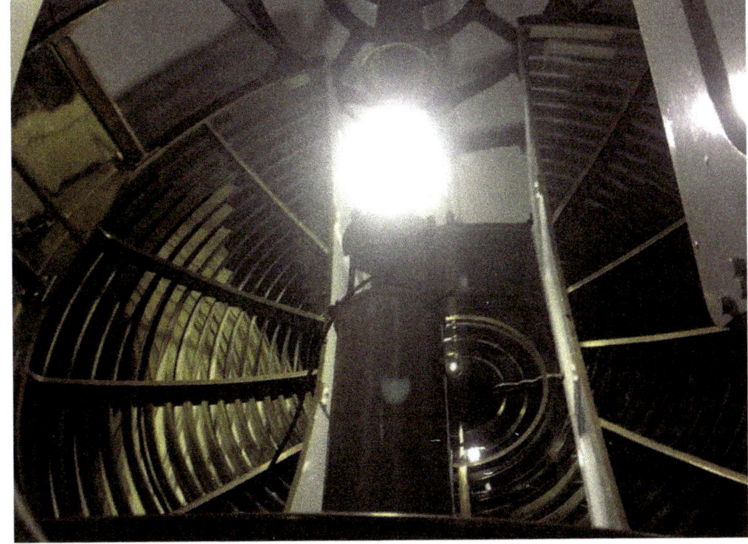

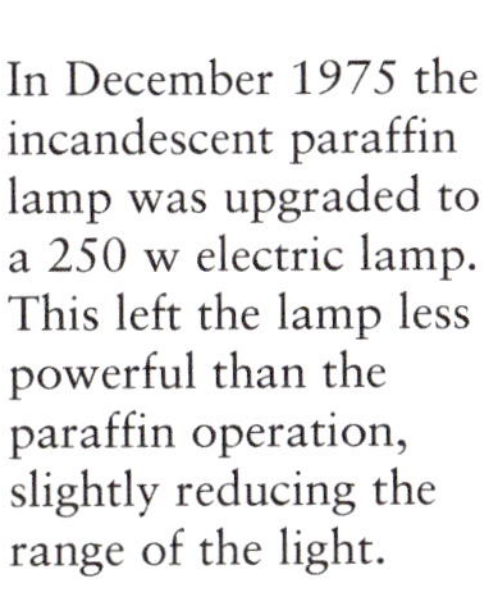

In December 1975 the incandescent paraffin lamp was upgraded to a 250 w electric lamp. This left the lamp less powerful than the paraffin operation, slightly reducing the range of the light.

His frustration at this is understandable considering that for as long as paraffin was burned, the lens would require cleaning every morning (or perhaps every second morning in the summer) and the paraffin cans would require carrying to the top of the tower.

While the commissioners appear to have taken no notice of Mr McDonald's gentle request for an electric light, they did eventually upgrade the lamp in December 1975 (by which time McDonald had gone). The electric lamp would reduce the cleaning burden on the keepers, for the lens would now require only light cleaning once weekly. The electric operation, which used a 250 w mercury vapour lamp, was also more reliable and meant the keepers would no longer need to periodically pump the paraffin tanks to keep the light burning. It did, however, reduce the strength of the lighthouse to about 640,000 candlepower. With electricity the lamps were now more reliable than the mantle-lit paraffin variety, but things could still go wrong. After electrification one Supernumerary fell asleep at his post, causing the light to stand – the worst offence a keeper could commit. The Principal felt bad at having to report the apprentice, but if he failed to report it he knew a fishing boat probably would. The Supernumerary told the Principal not to feel bad for reporting him as he was fed up with the work anyway!

Arriving at Kinnaird with a young family, Mr John Boath, Assistant Lightkeeper from 1975 to 1978, described the station as a 'five star hotel' compared to most lighthouses. He has fond memories of Fraserburgh, because when off duty he was able to easily go for a stroll around the town, popping in to visit friends. It even provided a second job, delivering Calor gas to fishing boats down in the harbour. The town also provided a better social life for him and his wife as they were able to go for nights out and with neighbours in Castle Terrace they were never short of babysitters! The children too had good memories of Kinnaird, whether it be playing on the shore, whelking for extra pocket money or playing with friends at the Wine Tower. If their friends did stay over at the lighthouse, they were often given the treat of being able to wind the clockwork machine for the keepers who were happy to allow them to undertake the work.

In July 1980 Principal Keeper Jimmy Shanks and his family arrived at the station after transfer from Langness on the Isle of Man. His wife Lily and daughters Eileen and Elayne had been with him almost from the very beginning his career, Lily recalling that when she arrived at her first station at Holy Isle, Arran, in 1959 she thought she would last three weeks; they only had two paraffin lamps for lighting the house and a poor supply of water!

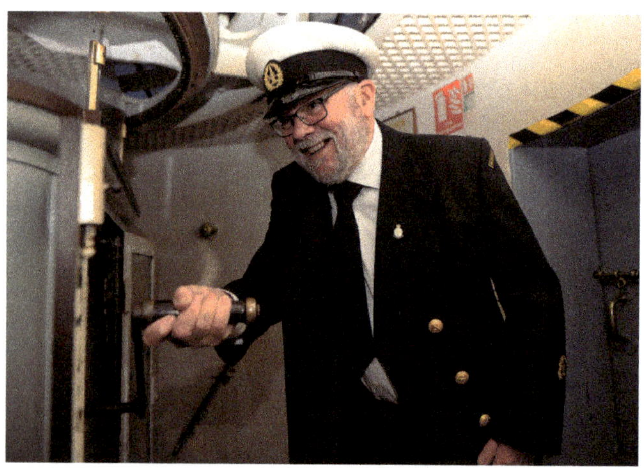

John Boath, assistant lightkeeper at Kinnaird Head 1975–78, returned to the lightroom in 2018 to commemorate the twentieth anniversary of automation. Mr Boath was the last principal lightkeeper of the Bell Rock. (Ian Cowe)

Twenty years later, Fraserburgh was a more welcome posting for her: 'It was handy – the shops were accessible and it was easy to get about. You could have a normal life.' For youngest daughter Elayne, in fourth year of high school and in among O-levels, the move was less welcome. As they reached the grey town of Fraserburgh, Lily recalled her teenage daughter's 'face was trippin' her all the way up in the car.' Upon arrival she stayed in her room for four days solid. Unfortunately her choice of O-levels at her previous high school clashed on the timetable at Fraserburgh Academy, meaning she had to drop her first choice of subjects. Further, as Elayne explains, 'leaving friends behind in primary school didn't bother you, but it was different in high school.' Making new friends in Fraserburgh would initially prove challenging for both sisters, thanks in no small part to their difficulty in understanding the local Doric dialect. It is clear the transfer did have an impact on their studies, but Lily adds: 'It didn't do any of them any harm. They both got good jobs.'

While the station would become a happy home for the family, one thing they distinctly remembered were the ghosts. Elayne's room, a converted coal store, was next to the sitting room. One winter morning she noticed that all the baubles had been taken off the Christmas tree and gathered at the other side of the room. They had no indoor pets. In Eileen's room, which was described by some visitors as 'creepy' and always cold, the bed would often move during the day. On another occasion when the family were in the sitting room they heard a clatter in the bathroom and upon investigating they found that a porcelain plaque that usually hung on the door had been smashed off the opposite wall. To this day they have no other explanation for how this could have happened,

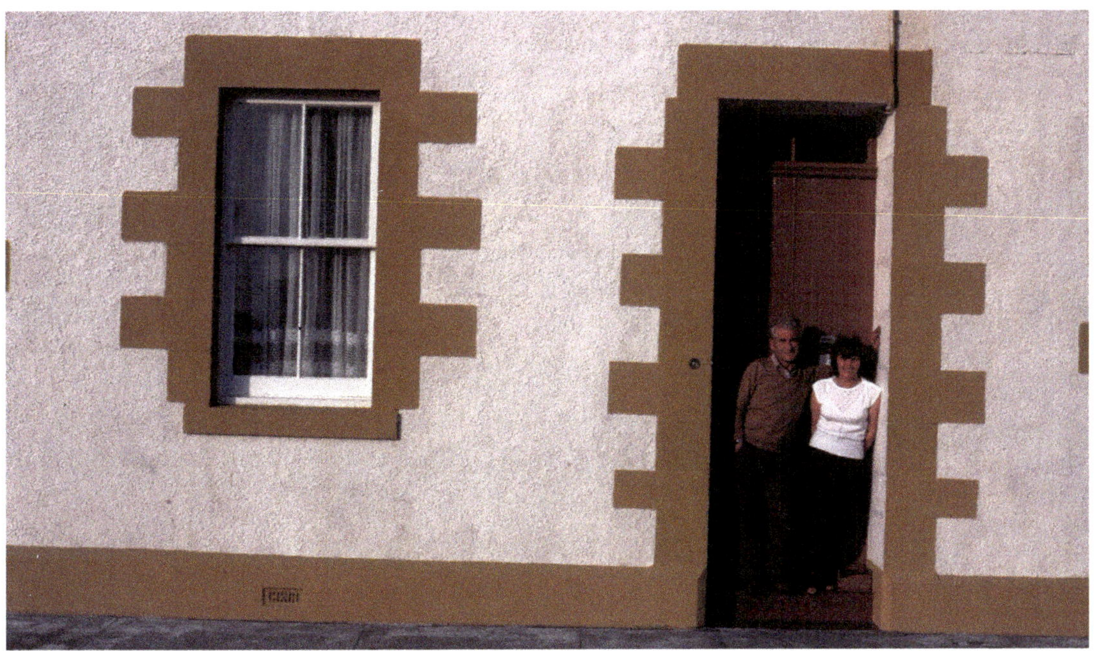

Jimmy Shanks, principal keeper 1980–86, with his wife Lily at the principal keeper's house at Kinnaird Head *c.* 1986. Jimmy painted the cottages in the mustard and white without consent from the commissioners – they had been grey and white. He feared he would be disciplined but the superintendent liked the new colour scheme so much that they started using it at other stations. (Allardyce Collection, Museum of Scottish Lighthouses)

other than something paranormal. They were not alone: Assistant Lightkeeper Bill Gault was woken one evening in his own cottage by the ghost of a woman, the Shanks recalling it took him some time before he was comfortable speaking about the experience. These hauntings seemed to last only a couple of years before normality resumed.

Mr Shanks was one of the last career keepers to be based at Kinnaird Head, and among the last of the true paraffin oilers. He served in the era of men being winched on to rock stations by pully: 'He knew what it was like to be a fish on a hook.' Near the end of his service, Kinnaird Head offered him none of those hardships but quality family time with no need for radio-telephones. He was keen on arts and crafts, woodworking and was expert in making ships in bottles. Perhaps his prize at Kinnaird Head was the garden: 'Jimmy had green fingers, but not for flowers.' His garden at Kinnaird grew marrows, rhubarb, potatoes, tomatoes, strawberries and even grapes in the greenhouse. This highlighted one drawback of living in a town as the local lads were known to pinch from his garden! The family were the second to last to be transferred away from Kinnaird Head as Jimmy was sent to Sanda lighthouse on the west coast, Lily following him to Oban. He would see that lighthouse made automatic, before being sent to Rhinns of Islay. His family see him as one of the lucky ones: he retired from the service before compulsory redundancies became the norm. As for Elyane, so sorry to be taken to Fraserburgh six years earlier, she stayed behind in the town for a period, Kinnaird Head being her last lighthouse home. Despite the hardships of growing up in the service, like the rest of the family, she was saddened at approaching automation which would bring about the end of their way of life: 'You never realised how unique your upbringing was until you had grown up. It was a happy childhood.'

Soon after the Shanks were moved on there was another big step towards automation at Kinnaird with the discontinuance of the foghorn in November 1987. The foghorn, as a technology, was seen to be outdated. It had effectively been superseded by the radio beacon in 1929 and further still with advancements in radar beacons through the twentieth century. With most stations due to be de-manned in the coming decade, it was not economical to have the horns automated as they annoyed the locals on land while the skippers at sea, increasingly looking at radar in their modern wheelhouses, could no longer hear them. As a result a number of horns were silenced at the same time in 1987, bringing to an end the mournful sound of Fraserburgh's Castle Coo.

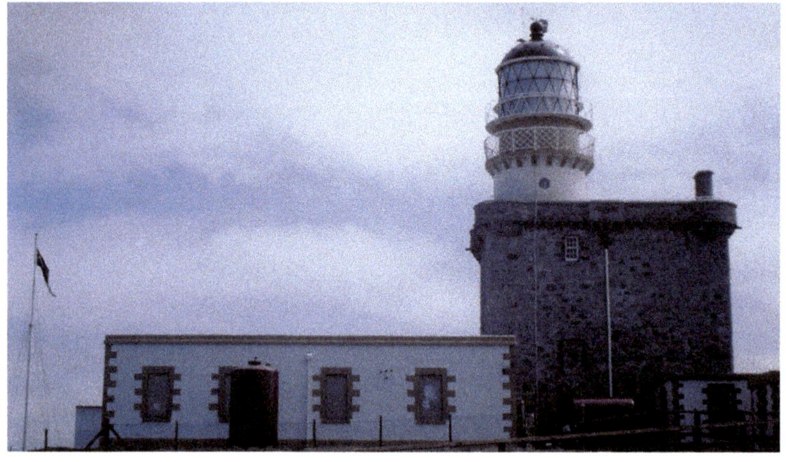

In 1987 the foghorn was discontinued. In this image the engine room windows can be seen boarded up, the building falling out of use *c.* 1990.

Just over six months later, in May 1988, James B. Oliver was posted to Kinnaird Head to take over the duties of Principal Keeper. Mr Oliver, who served twenty-six years as a keeper, was a traditional paraffin oiler himself – his father Robert serving as a career keeper before him. By the time he arrived it was already known that his new station was gearing up for automation with plans being put in place for the lighthouse. It must have begun to feel real in October 1990 when the foundations of a new, smaller tower were built to the north of the old lighthouse in place of the now outdated radio mast. The keepers, attending to their duties, watched as this modern 10-metre-tall fibreglass lighthouse quickly rose from its foundations. They were daily face-to-face with the technology that would make them, and the historic light, redundant.

At 4:08 hours on the morning of Friday June 21 1991, Principal Keeper Jim Oliver turned off the operational light at Kinnaird Head for the last time. With that simple and quick action, and no fanfare, he brought to an end the 204 years of manned service at Kinnaird Head. All three keepers, Jim Oliver, Ernest England and Sam Wilson, were now redundant. With so few lights still manned there were no more vacancies and nowhere for them to go. Later that evening they watched as the new light took over their nightly vigil and the new age of automation began at Kinnaird Head.

Speaking in 2009, Mr Oliver reflected on the end of the manned service: 'I was born into the lighthouse service … and if it wasn't for the way things had changed there's a fair chance that my son would have followed me.' By 1998 all of Scotland's lighthouses would be automated. Despite the strict discipline of the service, the comparatively low wages and the remote locations of the stations, it was an occupation and a way of life loved by many, including Mr Oliver: 'If things changed back and they wanted the lighthouse manned again, I'd be right there at the head of the queue.'

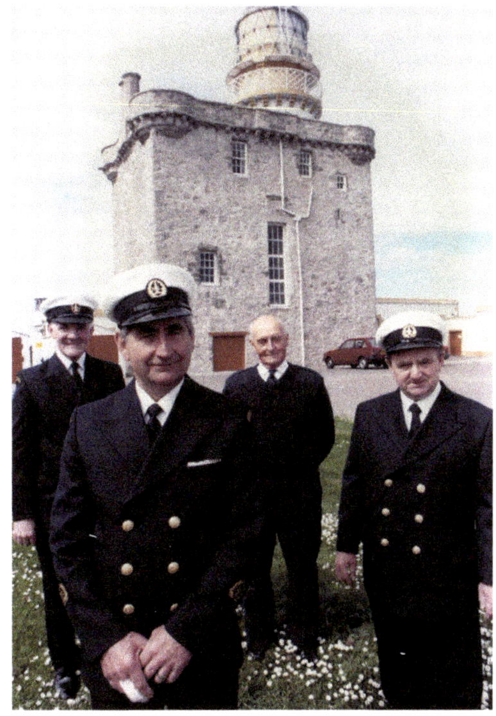

On 21 June 1991 the historic lighthouse at Kinnaird Head was decommissioned due to automation, and the keepers withdrawn. Pictured are the last keeper (left to right): Ernest England, principal lightkeeper Jim Oliver, Willie Hansen and S. P. Wilson. (Aberdeen Journals)

Chapter 10

Automation and Afterlife

Automation

The new automatic light at Kinnaird Head was not, at first, well received by the fishermen and mariners who depended on it. In March 1992 it was noted that the light 'appears to lack a sharpness to its flash which contributes to the definition as any cars in the same vicinity all appear much brighter.' Even the old Principal Keeper Jim Oliver, as attendant keeper to the new lighthouse, was receiving complaints, as he informed the Board: 'Since the light at Kinnaird Head was automated a number of fishing boat Skippers have made complaint to me that the new light is not very clear, and at times indistinguishable against the background of the town.' The skippers had presented

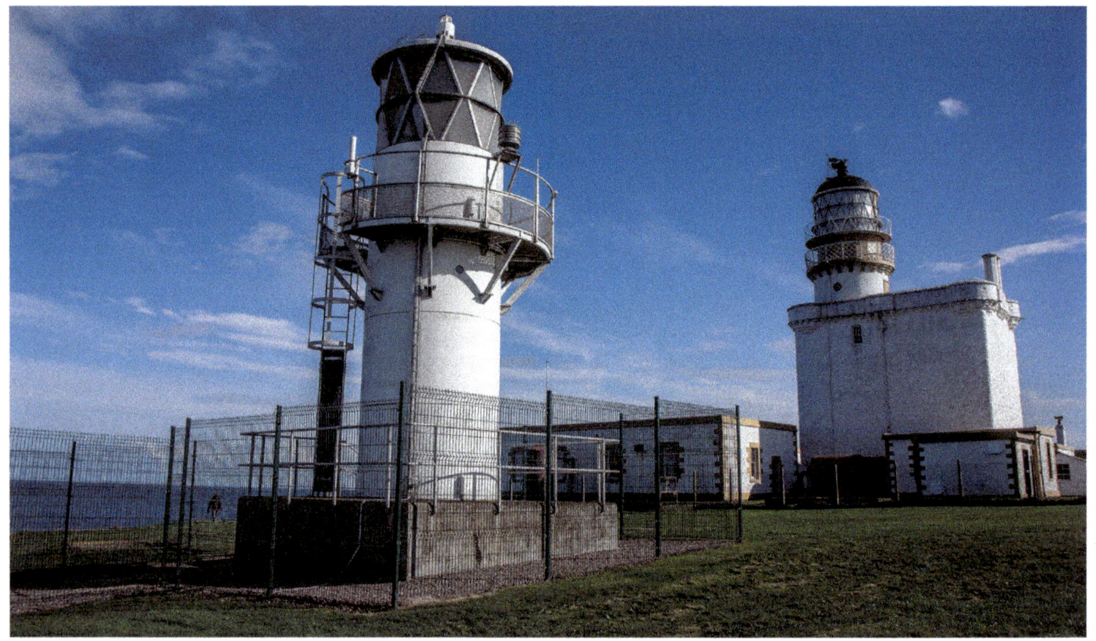

The new automatic lighthouse, now monitored from Edinburgh, came into operation in June 1991. (Billy Watson)

Mr Oliver with a signed letter for the attention of the commissioners. The letter, signed by thirteen skippers, highlighted that they paid on average £350 on lighting dues every year for only three lights in their immediate vicinity; they expected better. The content of the complaint highlighted that due to car headlights in two main carparks it was impossible to tell where the light was from the sea: 'It is imperative therefore that a light is created in order that the head can be seen in the dark, or that the power of the replacement light be increased so the light is distinguishable.'

MV *Pole Star*, one of the lighthouse ships, was dispatched to investigate the complaint and ultimately agreed that 'background lighting and road vehicle headlights' were interfering with the visibility of the new lighthouse. The Master of the *Pole Star* noted that the most direct way of improving the situation would be to increase the height of the light by adding more fibreglass sections but warned this would also be the most costly solution. A second and much cheaper solution would be if 'the character of the light should be drastically altered to counter the 'car effect'.

The Board immediately set about improving the situation by first increasing the brilliancy of the main optic 'by bringing two further sealed beam lamps into play', but tests in June 1992 found in favour of the Master of the *Pole Star*'s suggestion of speeding up the flash sequence. The character of the light was to change from a flash every fifteen seconds, to a flash every five seconds, with the improved brilliancy ensuring the light was more distinguishable with a nominal range of twenty-two miles. This was the first alteration to the character of the station since 1903. The proposed change did create another headache for the Board. The flash at Kinnaird Head was now deemed to be too similar to the Cairnbulg Beacon's white flash every three seconds. To further resolve this situation the Cairnbulg Beacon's character was to be altered to a group flash of two white every ten seconds on 12 August 1992, while the proposed change at Kinnaird Head would occur on 16 December 1992. These major issues must have given some satisfaction to the now redundant keepers, but thankfully since these early issues were resolved there has been no other major issues with the new station.

Operation of Automatic Light

Even the automatic lights require some form of semi-regular human assistance. In the early days of automation this role was undertaken by an attendant keeper who was responsible for upkeep of the lighthouse on a one-man, one-light basis. As noted, the first attendant keeper of the new lighthouse was Mr Oliver who undertook the role of attendant for a number of years. All going well, the duties of the attendant should be light: attend to the lighthouse generally once every month to monitor the charge of batteries; clean the optic and lantern; undertake checks of emergency lighting etc. There is no requirement for the attendant to 'watch' the light as all lighthouses in Scotland – since 1998 – are now 'watched' from the NLB's monitoring centre at their HQ, 84 George Street Edinburgh. If there is any failure with the lighthouse it will flag up on the computer and will be dealt with centrally. If it cannot be dealt with from Edinburgh, the attendant or a technician may be called to check on or fix the light.

The current attendant at Kinnaird Head is seventy-six-year-old Mr Gordon Stewart, who now has the title Retained Lightkeeper (RLK), despite the fact he was never a serving keeper. His service with the NLB started in 1981 supplying Rattray Head, a role he

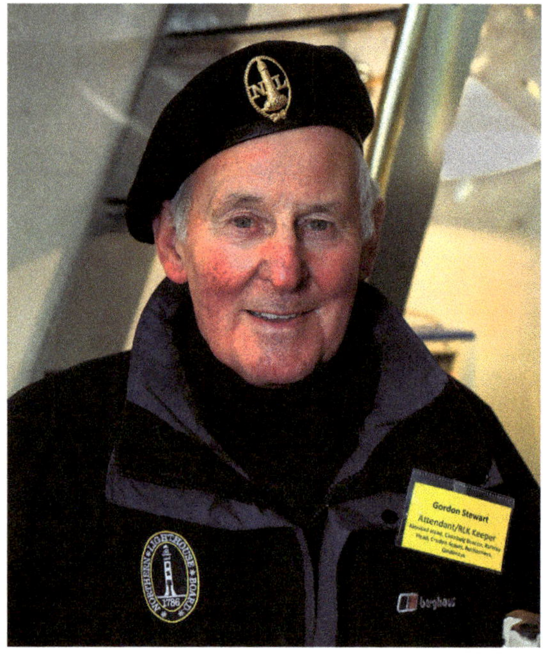

Mr Gordon Stewart, retained lightkeeper, visits the automatic lighthouse at least once a month to ensure its continued brilliancy. (Mark Grant)

says was only supposed to be temporary job … thirty-seven years ago! His knowledge of attending to the Rattray Head lighthouse secured his position as the NLB changed from a system of one-man, one-light, to one man covering an area. That is the distinction between an attendant and an RLK. With this change Mr Stewart became responsible for four major lights and two beacons between Kinnaird Head and Girdleness. Mr Stewart has no plans to retire, stating that with advancements in Health and Safety the job has become less and less difficult: 'We're not even supposed to clean the window panes these days as nature takes care of that – you're not allowed to do so much stretching above your head.' The job is not always so relaxed, as in 2018 Mr Stewart was pulled over by anti-terrorism police due to his frequent journeys to Rattray Head and Cruden Scaurs. These two lights just happen to be close by to one of the largest gas terminals in the UK at St Fergus, Aberdeenshire.

The lights rarely fail. The main optic consists of two lenses on top of each other, each with their own bulb. If one bulb were to fail, the second would still be in action as a back-up but, again, with LED lights this rarely happens nowadays. The lens, incidentally, continually rotates on its gearless pedestal because it does not know anything other than light and dark, which is indicated to the light by means of photoelectric cell. The lens must always have a constant rotation to produce the correct flash. If there was a failure with the main optic, the electrical current would automatically be redirected to two emergency lights located at either side of the main optic. Both work independently with their own photoelectric cell sensors and will produce the same character as the failed main optic: one flash white every five seconds. Even if there is a power cut to the mains electric the light will continue as it is hooked up to a back-up supply of batteries, which will keep the light operating long enough for any fault to be repaired.

Like the old light, the new light also requires upgrades at regular intervals – normally every ten years or so. In 2019 the lighthouse was given its most comprehensive upgrade since 1991 with the renewal of the lantern glass and emergency optics.

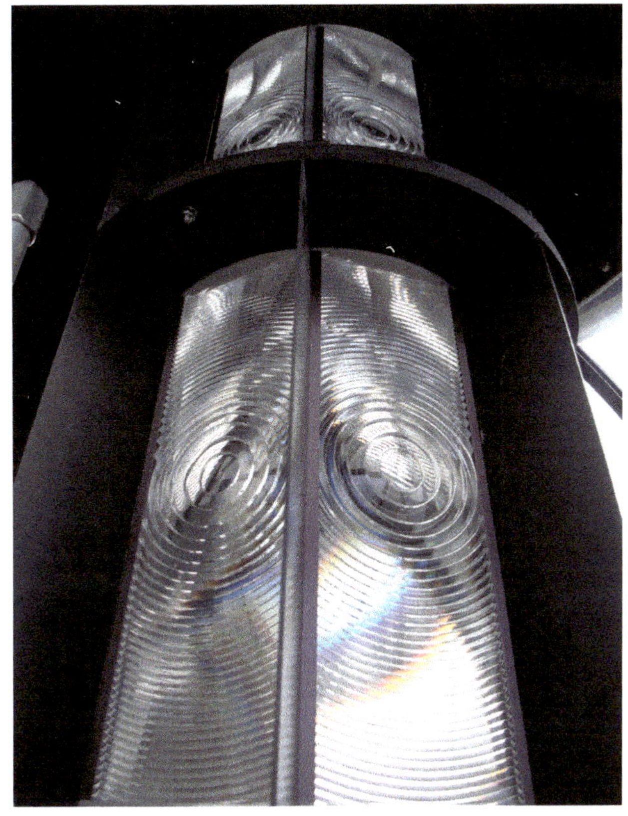

Right: The optic is now made of plastic and is much smaller than in the old light, being of the 4th Order size. There are two optics, meaning that if one lamp failed the other would still continue to flash. (Northern Lighthouse Board)

Below: If the main optic failed entirely, power would be directed to two emergency lights located on either side of the lantern. These LED lights will give the same character as the main optic, although the range is reduced to 12 miles.

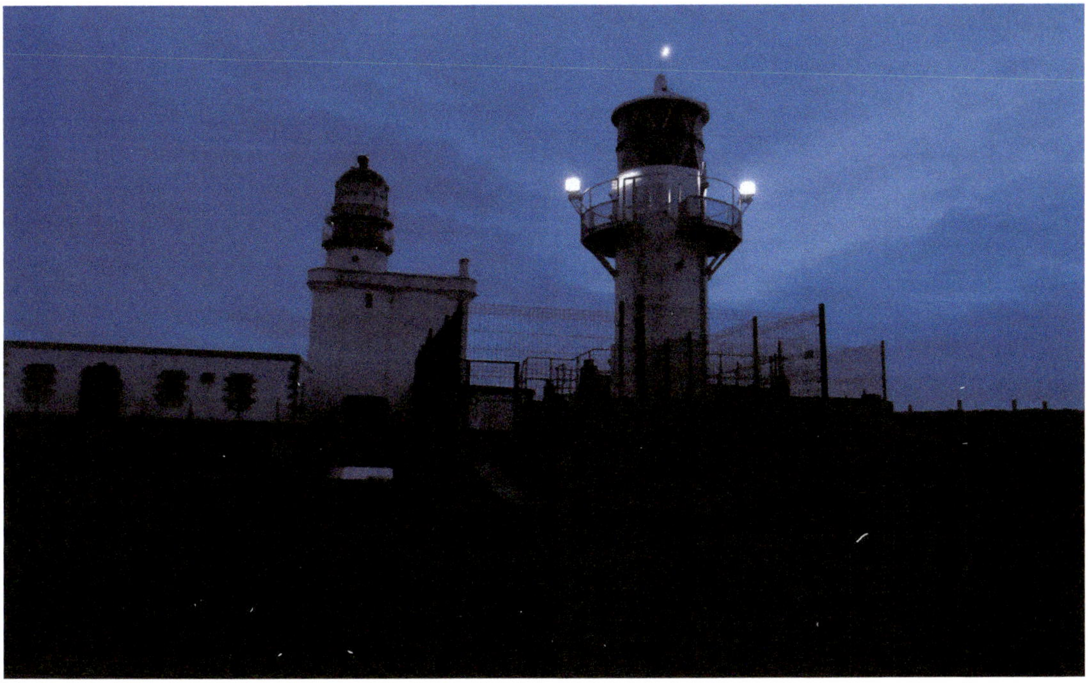

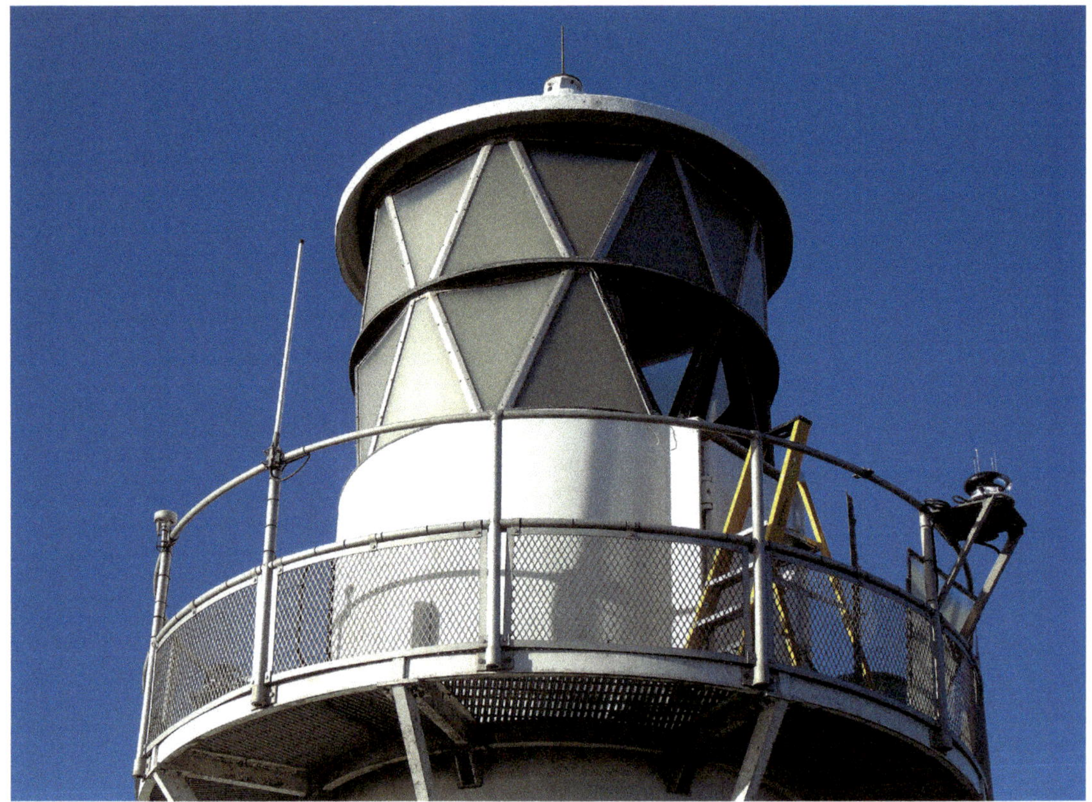

At the time of writing (March 2019) the automatic light is undergoing an upgrade to replace the lantern glass and update the emergency lights. The light undergoes an upgrade usually every ten years.

Afterlife

Under normal circumstances there would have been no need for a purpose-built, automatic lighthouse at Kinnaird Head. Had the normal protocols of automation been followed a new light would have been established in the existing tower, the lens and mechanism being removed and the lantern fitted with new optical equipment. In the case of Kinnaird the magnificent hyper-radial lens would most likely have been replaced with a sealed beam unit, which is effectively a revolving line of car headlights. By the late 1980s this routine had played out over most of Scotland's lighthouses, to the extent that the Northern Lighthouse Board now had a surplus of redundant lenses in their stores in Edinburgh and at Inchkeith lighthouse. Kinnaird Head was, as mentioned in the introduction, to be the exception to this rule as the managers at 84 George Street advanced an ambitious alternative course for their first lighthouse.

As early as April 1988 the NLB General Manager (formerly Secretary) and Engineer were already having discussions about a 'Possible museum at Kinnaird Head'. It seems likely this idea had been born of the NLB's bi-centenary in 1986, which celebrated their unique heritage, as well as the realisation that by 1998 there would be no serving lightkeepers left in Scotland with the conclusion of the automation programme. The NLB's plan for the museum was small in scale at this stage, the museum being contained within the cottages and tower of Kinnaird Head lighthouse: 'There are several buildings which can be utilised for the purposes of providing a museum at Kinnaird Head.' In these buildings Engineer Bill Paterson proposed that equipment could be exhibited, even going as far to suggest that he could approach the Marine Superintendent to see if he had any redundant buoys which 'could be placed around the courtyard.' Central to the plan was, however, the idea of the lighthouse tower and foghorn being kept exactly as they were, preserved to represent the age of the Lightkeeper into the twenty-first century.

Four months later, in August 1988, Grampian Regional Council had the first meeting of a working group focussed on what was now a joint venture to create a museum championing Scotland's lighthouses and the work of the Northern Lighthouse Board. At this first meeting the possibility of 'obtaining additional space outwith the lighthouse property' for the museum was raised, the initial thoughts being such a space could be used to exhibit the lenses in NLB storage. Mr Paterson wrote to the General Manager: 'It is highly desirable that these lenses and those yet to be removed should be put on display where the fine optical engineering can be appreciated by many rather than have them hidden away in Tower Street Lane [Edinburgh].' The proposal got the go ahead, and measures were then taken to establish Scotland's Lighthouse Museum Ltd, an independent body which would manage the new museum.

It was by no means an easy task. The initial plan was to have the museum open by 1992 to coincide with the Fraserburgh 400 Celebrations, that being the 400th anniversary of Sir Alexander Fraser's Burgh. The site was originally supposed to be taken into the care of the National Trust for Scotland but the deal fell through with a change of leadership at the Trust, putting the whole project in jeopardy. After all, when did anything ever go entirely to plan in the castle's 400-year history? Meanwhile the NLB instructed Mr Oliver to do what he could to increase the number of tours of his lighthouse as a means of proving how lighthouses held the interest of the public and could attract visitors. Whether it was Mr Oliver's tours or something else, the property eventually entered the care of Historic Scotland, safeguarding the future of Kinnaird Head lighthouse as an historic monument.

Scotland's Lighthouse Museum

Since June 1995 Kinnaird Head lighthouse has been managed by, and is an important part of, the Museum of Scottish Lighthouses. The museum's main building sits on the former grounds of Kinnaird Head about 150 yards from the lighthouse complex. This building became home to the NLB's collection of redundant lenses, all of which have been donated to the independent museum. Since its inception the first manager, Richard Townsley, set ambitious plans for the museum as not only would it host the redundant lenses, but a complete national collection of lighthouse artefacts. He traversed a great many of Scotland's lighthouses, earmarking pieces he wished to acquire for the collection in Fraserburgh, with the NLB giving either a yay or a nae. By 2007 the whole collection was granted the acclaimed status of being a Recognised Collection of National Significance, that meaning its depth is great enough to paint the entire national picture of Scotland's lighthouses. Today, under the management of Lynda McGuigan, the museum continues to attract an average of 30,000 people per year to the town of

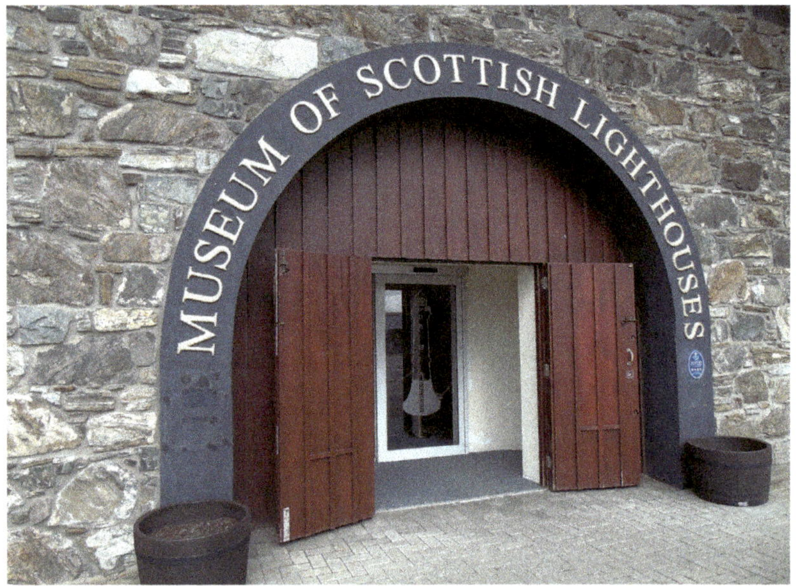

The Museum of Scottish Lighthouses, which includes the old Kinnaird Head Lighthouse, opened in 1995 giving new life to the historic site.

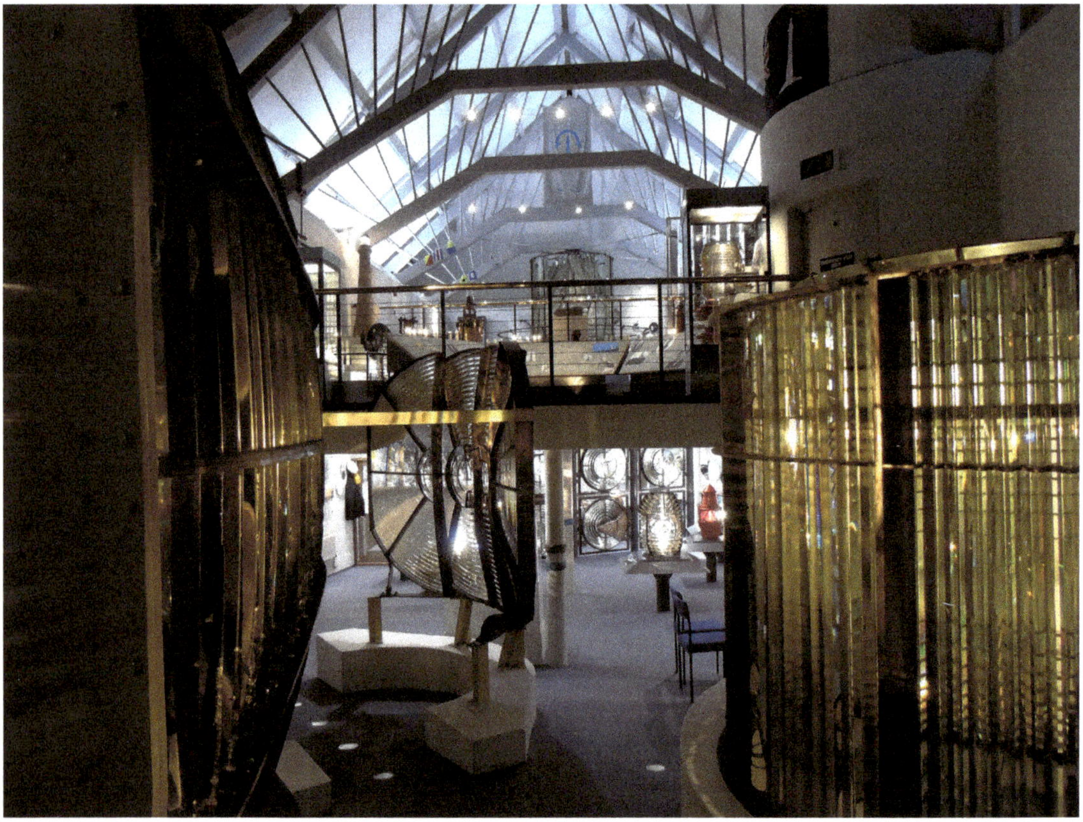

The museum holds a Recognised Collection of National Significance, principally made up of 'redundant' lenses donated by the Northern Lighthouse Board.

Fraserburgh. This is no mean feat considering it is not somewhere you travel through or arrive at by chance. With the decline of the fishing, tourism is an ever-important market for the area, the museum doing its part to contribute to the local community.

All this has been possible simply because of Kinnaird Head lighthouse, the mother light of the Northern Lighthouse Board. Despite the acclaimed museum it is acknowledged by staff that the majority of visitors come to the museum simply because they want to visit the historic lighthouse. That is the draw of the site. For twenty-five years a team of dedicated guides have taken hundreds of thousands of visitors up Robert Stevenson's open staircase, telling them of Kinnaird Head's unique history and its place within the Northern Lighthouse Board. The tour guides have acted as the modern keepers of the old lighthouse. They play their part, serve the light, and more often than not, move on. The difference between then and now is the old lighthouse had the purpose of keeping ships away from the headland, while in its new capacity that same light is used to attract visitors from all around the globe to the town of Fraserburgh.

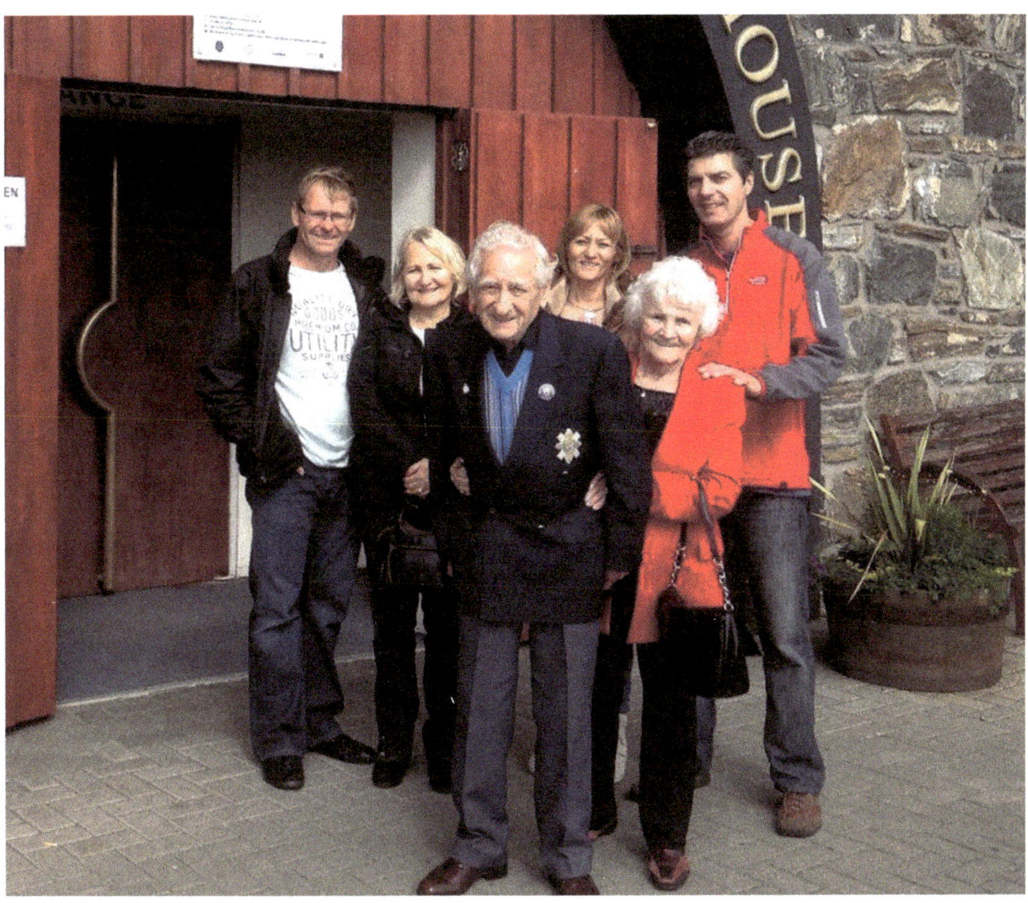

The museum has become a place of pilgrimage for many lighthouse families. Former principal lightkeeper Jimmy Shanks (1931–2016), his wife Lily and daughters Eileen and Elayne visited their former home at Kinnaird Head in 2014 as part of Jimmy's final tour of his former stations. Even as dementia set in, his family say 'the lighthouse service never left him.'

Conclusion

As has been shown in this book, Kinnaird Head has always been the exception to the rule in the history of Scottish lighthouses. In the first instance, the lighthouse was built on top of – and then through the middle of – a sixteenth-century castle. This fact alone is enough to make the lighthouse unique in the world. It is this exceptionalism and accident of history that most likely prevented Sir Alexander Fraser's castle from falling into total ruin, to survive to the present date. This exceptionalism presented itself not only at the beginning of its existence as a lighthouse, but also at the end of that history when it escaped the fate of all others by avoiding the normal automation process.

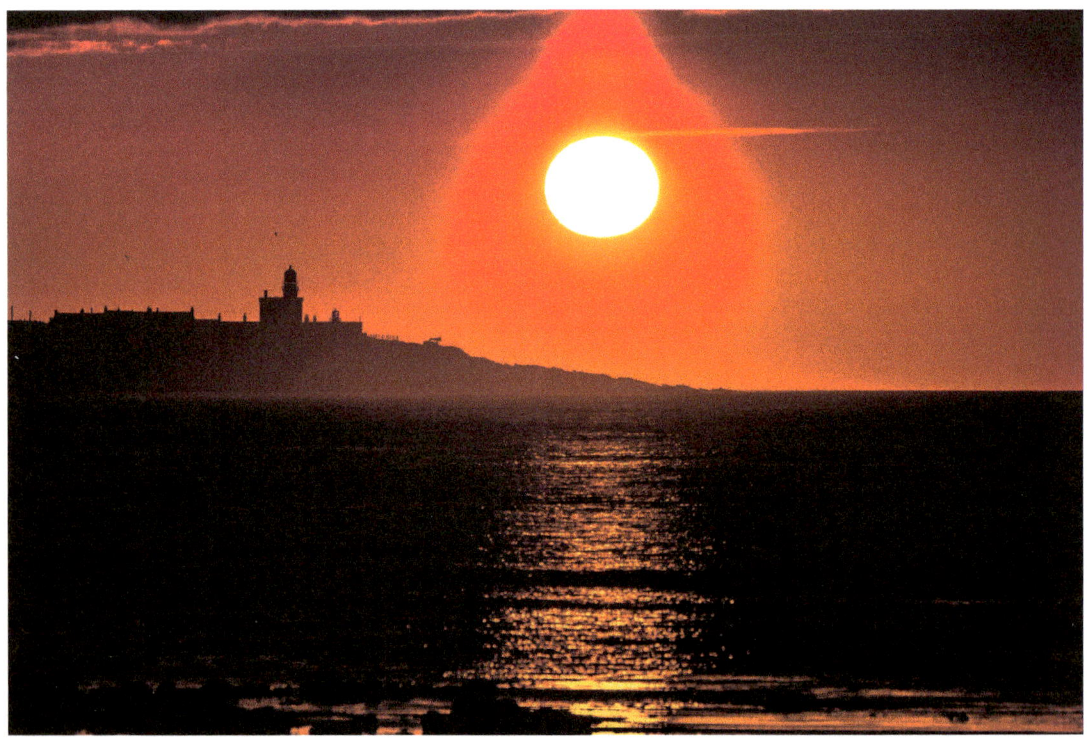

Sunset at Kinnaird Head, from Cairnbulg harbour. (Billy Watson)

As it did in 1787, Kinnaird Head once again stands alone as the only lighthouse in Scotland in a permanent manned state. It has reinvented itself once more in order to preserve itself for a new purpose.

What is equally extraordinary is that, within the context of this exceptionalism among lighthouses, on an operational level it was no different to all the others. It was built and altered by the same engineers who served the other Northern Lighthouses and attended to by the same hundreds of keepers who, with their families, were transferred across the length and breadth of the country many times over to serve all of Scotland's lighthouses. In many respects it is this typicality that has ultimately made the lighthouse so important today; it may have a unique and interesting story in its building and rebuilding, but it has become an important historical site for highlighting the everyday lives of the lightkeepers. For over 204 years Kinnaird Head – between Jim Park and Jimmy Oliver – was served by 32 Principal Lightkeepers and countless Assistants, Supernumeraries and Occasionals. The building survives today more as a monument to them over any other factor: it is a monument to a lost way of life.

The author has had the immense privilege to work in the old tower of Kinnaird Head on an almost daily basis for seven years (give or take) in its most recent incarnation as a museum. While this book gives perhaps the best account of the lighthouse to date, it cannot compare to the atmosphere of the actual tower. The smell of paraffin clings to the very fabric of the building even today, occasionally being overpowered by the

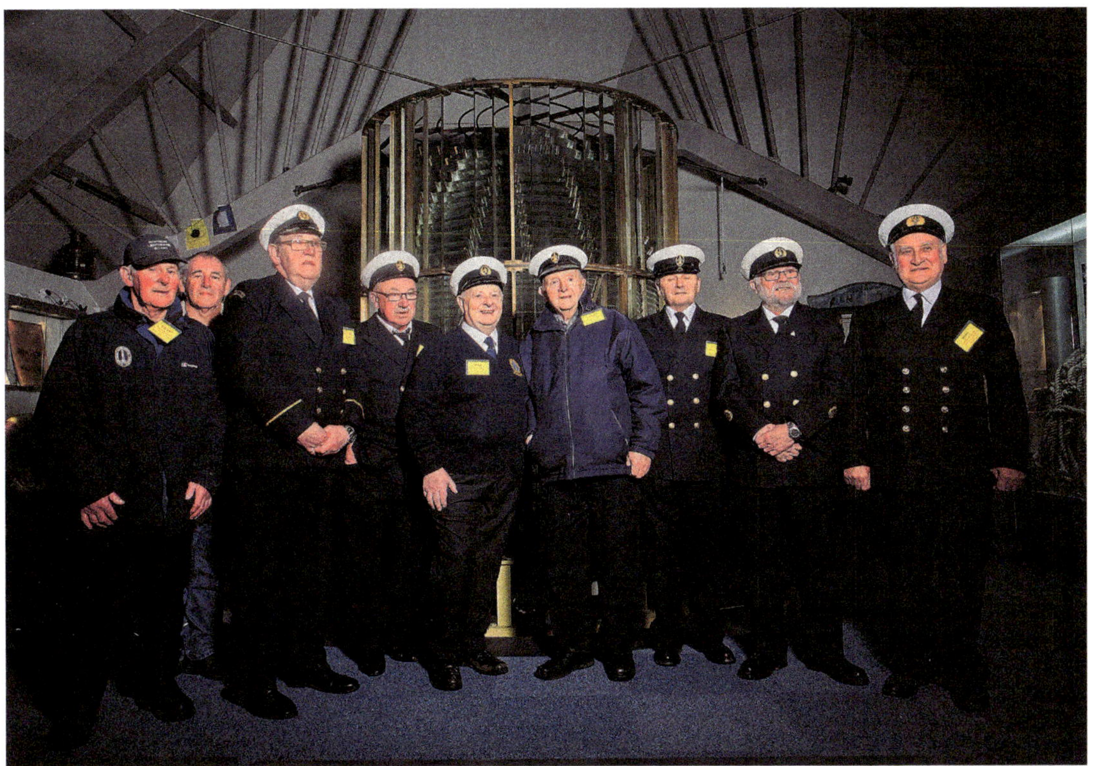

In March 2018 retired lightkeepers returned to Kinnaird Head to man the lighthouse for one night to commemorate the twentieth anniversary of national automation. (Mark Grant)

smell of Brasso from the lightroom. The sound of the 1902 clockwork machine can be heard ticking down Stevenson's tower and while the history of this extraordinary place is recounted to visitors, the ghosts of some of those mentioned in this book can be imagined going about their daily business in the very spaces where you stand. Owned and preserved by Historic Environment Scotland, Kinnaird Head, as the working example, has been the Museum of Scottish Lighthouses' greatest tool in educating thousands of visitors about the keepers and the mission of the Northern Lighthouse Board in illuminating the coasts of Scotland for the safety of all. It has, though, also become an important place for the community of Fraserburgh.

With the establishment of the museum, history has come full circle: the castle, as Sir Alexander Fraser always intended, is once again the recognised symbol of the town of Fraserburgh. Its benefits are not only economic, as it is clear that the building holds a special place in the heart of the community. It is a building looked to at special events as in recent years it has been central to local celebrations for the Queen's Diamond Jubilee (2012); it was illuminated in pink for the 'Moonlight Prowlers' who raised hundreds of thousands of pounds for breast cancer charities (2015); and more recently it projected a red poppy from the lantern to mark the 100th anniversary of the Armistice (2018).

By reinventing itself as a museum, Kinnaird Head has returned to its original purpose again, being seen as a symbol of hope, optimism and opportunity for the town. It is the Castle of Fraserburgh once more.

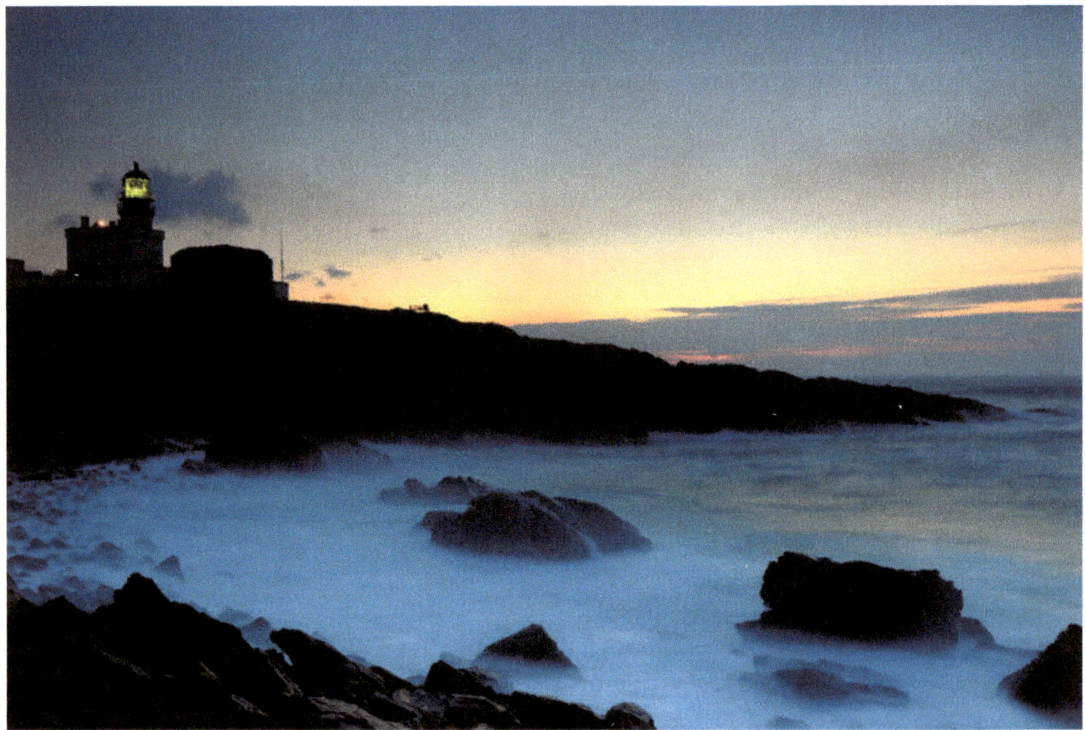

The lighthouse now serves as a centre of celebration and commemoration in the town of Fraserburgh, here being the focal point of the Queen's Diamond Jubilee in 2012. (Ian Cowe)

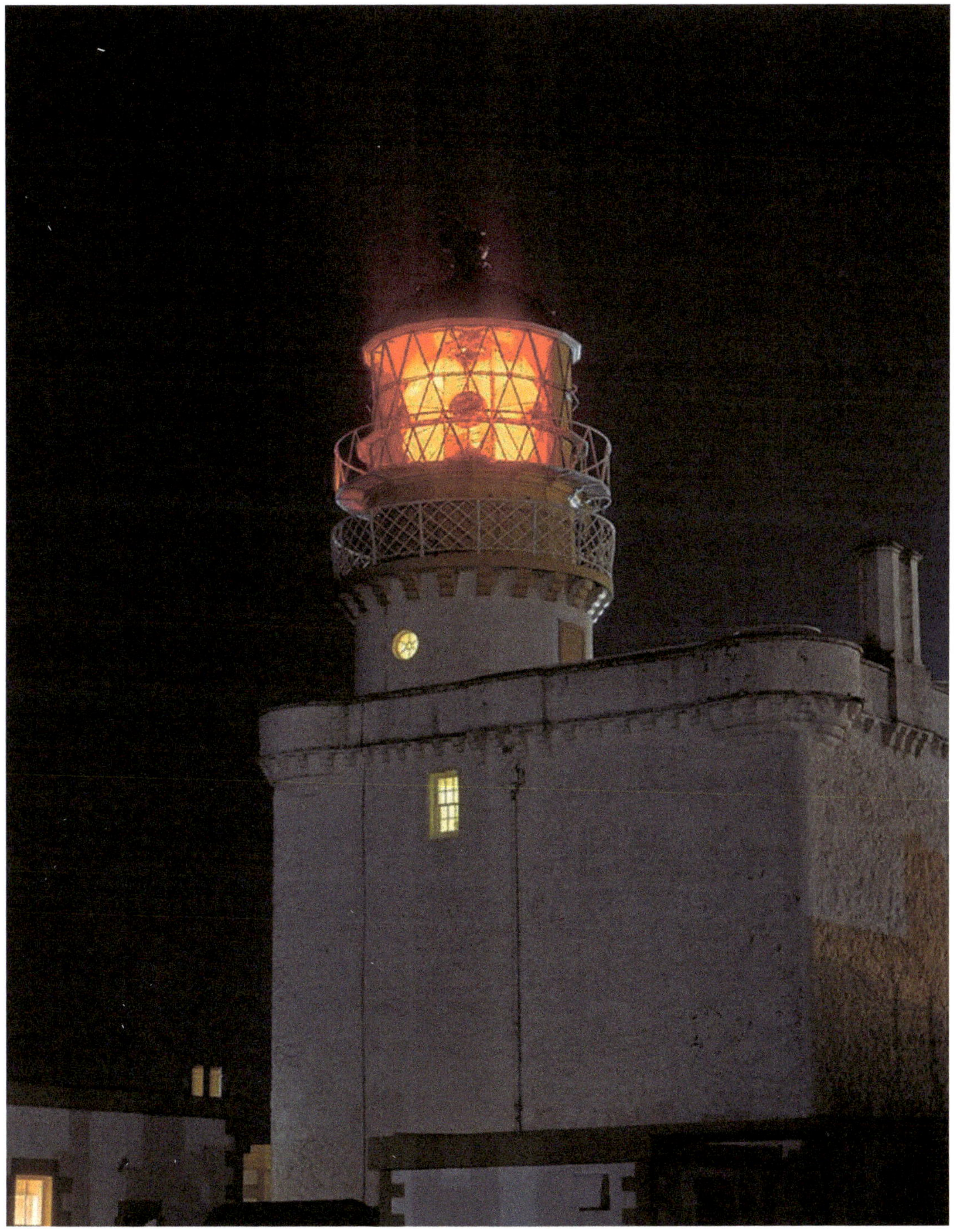

In November 2018 the hyper-radial lens shone a red poppy over Fraserburgh to commemorate the 100th anniversary of the end of the First World War. It was switched on by The Hon. Mrs Nicolson, direct descendant of Sir Alexander Fraser. (Mark Grant)

Select Bibliography

Fraser, A. (17th Lord Saltoun), *The Frasers of Philorth* (Edinburgh, 1879).
Morrison-Low, A. D., *Northern Lights: The Age of Scottish Lighthouses* (NMS, 2010).
Murison, Dr. D., *The Wine Tower* (1997).
Oram et al, *Historic Fraserburgh: Archaeology and Development* (Council for British Archaeology, 2010).
Stevenson, D. A., *The World's Lighthouses Before 1820* (Oxford University Press, 1959).
Swallow, S., *Kinnaird Head Lighthouse* (Scotland's Lighthouse Museum Trust, 1998).

Archive Materials

Business Records of Robert Stevenson & Sons, held at the National Library of Scotland, Edinburgh.
General Archives, held by Museum of Scottish Lighthouses, Fraserburgh.
Minute Books of the Commissioners of Northern Lighthouses, held by National Records Office, Edinburgh.
Papers of the Frasers of Philorth, held at Special Libraries and Archives, University of Aberdeen.